why I LOVE being CATHOLIC

DYNAMIC CATHOLIC AMBASSADORS SHARE
THEIR **HOPES** AND **DREAMS** FOR THE FUTURE

why I
LOVE
being
CATHOLIC

FOREWORD BY
MATTHEW KELLY

WELLSPRING
North Palm Beach, Florida

Design by Madeline Harris

ISBN 978-1-63582-062-1 (hardcover)
ISBN 978-1-63582-045-4 (softcover)
ISBN 978-1-63582-063-8 (ebook)

Library of Congress Control Number: 2018947141

Dynamic Catholic® and Be Bold. Be Catholic.® and The Best Version of
Yourself® are registered trademarks of The Dynamic Catholic Institute.

For more information on this title or other books and CDs available through the
Dynamic Catholic Book Program, please visit www.DynamicCatholic.com.

The Dynamic Catholic Institute
5081 Olympic Blvd • Erlanger • Kentucky • 41018
Phone: 1–859–980–7900
Email: info@DynamicCatholic.com

10   9   8   7   6   5   4   3   2   1

Printed in the United States of America

Contents

Foreword

vii

One

Why Do You Love Being Catholic?

1

Two

What Is Your Favorite Memory as a Catholic?

31

Three

As a Catholic, What Are Your Hopes for the Future?

125

Foreword

Matthew Kelly

People often ask me who I look up to, who my heroes are, who inspires me, and other varieties of these questions. They are always disappointed with my answer. They expect no doubt for me to name people everyone knows. I never do.

My heroes are the people who have contributed to this small volume, and millions more like them. The mere fact that you have picked this book up suggests that you are one of them.

My heroes are ordinary people, people who seek to live their one brief life with integrity and faith. They have dreams for themselves, their families, their church, and society. And they are serious about improving themselves, their families, their church, and society.

My heroes work hard to support their families. They volunteer in their parishes. They do what they can, with what they have, where they are, in order to bring a little more light into their corner of the world. They are lovers of a God who sometimes feels close, at other times seems to be far off and indifferent, and often seems elusive.

My heroes know their limitations. They have come face-to-face with their own inadequacies, and they know their faults and flaws better than most.

My heroes hold a common set of values that make them better people. And even though they fall short of these values on a daily basis, they wake up the next morning, dust themselves off, and strive again.

My heroes have money problems, marriage problems, and family problems. They strive to be the best parents they can be. They struggle with addiction, health problems, and often wonder if they are on the right career path. They show up and keep showing up in every aspect of life despite their shortcomings and uncertainty.

My heroes know that life is difficult. They know the ups and downs, the joys and heartaches, but they wake up each morning hoping for the best and working to make the world a better place for my children and yours.

These are my heroes. They make me want to be a better person.

The quality of a person's life is easily measured by the quality of the people in his or her life. I have been blessed in so many ways in this life. The people who have surrounded me have played a significant role in blessing my life.

One of the many, many reasons I love being Catholic is that it has been in the context of our faith that God has surrounded me with people like you.

There are so many other things I could have written about to open this book. Catholicism is rich with history and mystery, but it is the people and our common humanity that most inspires me at this moment.

So, whoever you are, wherever you are, keep doing doing what you can, where you are, with what you have. Pour yourself into your parish, pour yourself into some ministry, dedicate yourself to your own spiritual growth, and together let's remind millions of people of the millions of reasons to love being Catholic.

One

Why Do You Love Being Catholic?

I feel such a profound peace when I go to Mass. As soon as I walk through the church doors, I can feel God's love engulf my inner self. It is a mixture of joy and peace that I cannot put into words. As I kneel to talk to my heavenly Father about my week and how I am so grateful that he never left my side for one second, I can tell him about all my problems and know he is listening to my every word. I am a lector at our church, and I read over the readings the night before to begin trying to picture what message God is relaying to me in the Scriptures. I go to Mass thirty minutes early to calm myself, but it doesn't matter—my heart starts to beat fast. I know it is because I am so excited that I am getting ready to relay a very important message to my brothers and sisters. There is this little voice inside of me that is saying, "I am with you, and you can do it." I love being Catholic because there are so many ways for me to show my love for the sick, the homeless, and the dying. But most of all it's knowing that I am doing all these things as God would want.

—*Wanda Jackson*

Catholicism just makes sense!
—*Mary Elizabeth Carrizales*

In July of 2008, I attended a Cursillo retreat. During the three-day retreat, I experienced a profound change of mind and heart, and for the first time since my childhood, I fell in love again with Catholicism. I love how God makes me aware of his gifts and challenges me to use these to help others.
—*Pat Ahearn*

At one point in my life, I became very confused and mixed up, and I left the Catholic Church for a while. But with the help of a few very dedicated Catholic friends who prayed for me, instructed me, and loved me back into the Church again, I am here to stay. As a priest told me once, "You used to have your mother's Catholic faith, but now you have made it your own."
—*Connie Beckman*

One of the reasons I love being Catholic is that when I immerse myself in the treasures of our faith, an insatiable hunger is created, a deep longing to draw closer to the Lord.
—*Lynn Marion*

I was raised in the Lutheran Church. When I was three years old, we moved to a rural western Kansas town that had been settled by Volga German Catholics. The area has some of the most beautiful Catholic cathedrals in America. Most of my friends and school-mates were Catholic. My family did not understand the Catholic faith, though, so we made fun of the "fish-eaters."

Fast-forward to my high school years; I started dating the girl who is now my wife and the love of my life. She was born, raised, and educated in the Catholic faith. Her family, immediate and extended, are all Catholic and some of the kindest people I have ever met. As I spent more time with her family, a song from my Lutheran Sunday school kept coming into my thoughts, "They Will Know We Are Christians by Our Love." This defined my wife's family and their philosophy on life. As our love grew, my grandmother made a comment to me: "That Susie is such a nice girl; too bad she is Catholic." I informed her that we were getting married and the wedding would be in the Catholic Church. She frowned and said she would not be attending, but she was there.

As we were going through our marriage preparation classes, I asked the priest if I needed to join the Church so I could marry this girl. He replied, "No, but we do believe the family is always stronger when both parents belong to the Church."

I had promised to join the Church when we started our family. When our son was born six years later, I still did not jump into the RCIA process. When he was about two years old, he asked, "Why doesn't Daddy go to Communion with us?" I realized the priest had been right, and I enrolled in RCIA, dreading the next nine months. To my surprise, it was one of the most fulfilling experiences of my life.

I love the Catholic Church because it has given us a faith foundation for our family that continues to grow as we now enjoy seeing our grandchildren grow in their Catholic faith every day.

—*Jim Mall*

I love being Catholic because I tried it the "other way" for almost thirty years. "Running around the barn" is the term I used for those years of trying to build a deeper relationship with Jesus Christ. New age teachings, metaphysics, big box churches and television evangelists, meditation practices, astrology, psychometry, yoga—I tried it all, but I never felt the "fire" I feel for Jesus since returning to Catholicism. One of the "pieces to the puzzle" upon my return was being handed Matthew Kelly's book *Rediscovering Catholicism* at Christmas Mass!
—*Mary Anne Linsell*

At a very sad and dark time in my life, attending Mass meant everything and more to me. I felt lost, alone, confused, upset, and sick to my stomach. Going to Mass gave me somewhere to go and something to do with my time. I needed to surround myself with people, and Mass was the perfect place to do that. I realized Jesus loves me even in my brokenness. It's during hard times like this I'm glad there is daily Mass and ritual to depend on.
—*Siobhan Peryer*

My sorority's motto was "the first and the finest." I think the same holds true for our Catholic faith. It can be traced all the way back to Jesus himself. What an honor to be part of the original Christian faith that has been passed down from generation to generation! I also love how we preserve so many symbols and sacraments that also lead back to the time of Christ. Our faith runs deeper than most rivers, and it's flowing full of rich traditions!
—*Sara Schad*

I love being Catholic because it grounds me in my life. No matter what challenges I have faced in life, my Catholic faith has always been there for me. I have been fired from big jobs, my career position has been unjustly eliminated, I have been threatened with personal lawsuits, and I have had my life threatened by undesirable characters. In each of those cases, my Catholic faith guided me to a better place. How could I not love being Catholic?

—*Bob Bestvina*

I love being Catholic because it fosters community. I can go anywhere in the world and follow the same rituals: the Mass parts, veneration of saints, and Catholic values. To me, community represents the beauty of Catholicism. While I enjoy focusing on my personal relationship with God, it's even better when I surround myself with other like-minded people in my community who embrace authentic Catholic values.

—*Deb Meyer*

I love being a Catholic for all sorts of reasons. I'm an avid reader of work-related technical literature, which has proven to be highly positive and impactful in my career of thirty-plus years. I'm also an avid reader of Catholic literature. Catholic literature keeps me well grounded and reminds me constantly of all the many reasons of why I love being Catholic.

Catholicism is the team to be on. Yes, we have had some good players and some bad players, but over time, the team is the one I want to belong to because it stands for what is good and what is right, with an ultimate goal that cannot be matched. This team has and continues to have superstars; some of the best and brightest people through the ages are Catholics. Being Catholic is a way of life that is kind, compassionate, and wholesome. I cannot imagine being anything else but Catholic. As the saying goes, Jesus is the reason!

—Jim Rives

On December 12, 2010, I was awakened at 3:30 a.m. by the ringing of the telephone. That feeling of dread instantly enveloped me as I struggled to hear the news of the tragic event that happened to my son only a few hours ago. It involved a car accident in which the driver had slid off the icy road while driving a car full of college kids home after a party.

Immediately, my husband and I got in the car and drove four hours to Roanoke Hospital, where our son was waiting to see us in the trauma unit. The long drive and the constant praying of the rosary prepared us to receive the news of his condition: a spinal cord injury which left him paralyzed from the waist down. We were actually astonished to see him for the first time. His body was bruised and his broken ribs were uncomfortable, but the one thing that was most noticeable was his spirit and his face, which was almost glowing. He kept reassuring us that he would be fine and not to worry about him.

It was Sunday morning, and since we were aware of the power of the Mass, we left our son, Kevin, and went to find the closest Catholic church, bringing two of his best friends with us. I can honestly tell you that we have never been as comforted as we were that day when we heard the words of Scripture. The first reading from Isaiah spoke about the lame leaping like a stag, followed by Psalm 146, which stated that the Lord gives sight to the blind and the Lord raises up those who are bowed down. The Gospel was about John the Baptist in prison and how he sent his disciples to Jesus to see if he was really the Messiah. Jesus said to them, "Go and tell John what you hear and see: the blind regain their sight, the lame walk, lepers are cleansed, the deaf hear. . . ." We sat in utter amazement as we listened to these words and the words of the priest who gave a lesson on waiting patiently.

It has been over seven years since the accident, and although there have been some unpleasant times, we have always been comforted by our Lord and stayed very close to him through prayer. We have been surrounded by a wonderful parish, which has helped us out through prayers and support. Our son is joyful in the midst of his suffering and receives many graces from going to daily Mass. He teaches in a Catholic school and embraces each day with such confidence and trust in the Lord. We are waiting for a miracle but know for certain that God is working through this and we can definitely trust in his plan.

Why do I love being a Catholic? I have learned from the Catholic Church and from reading the lives of the saints about what life is really about and how to navigate this life, which is only a pilgrimage. No matter how hard life can get, we know that God has something great in store for us in the end. While I am here I can ask for the graces that I need each day. I love the fact that I can go to Mass each day and visit him in the Adoration chapel and he will give me everything I need to meet each challenge. This gives me the confidence that God's will is what I want. On those days that seem a bit more difficult, I just have to say, "Jesus, I trust in you"!

—*Diane Dyer*

I love the guidance the Church provides on how to live life. Because of the teachings, I have avoided many pitfalls in my life, and risen above many issues and circumstances. When I got pregnant with our son (there were a number of medical issues), every doctor/person advised me to have an abortion. We were advised that our son would be born with many disabilities if the pregnancy went to term. I read. I studied. And I followed the Church's advice not to have an abortion. Our son was born—perfectly healthy. He is extremely intelligent, very caring, and now thirty-one, getting married in October. He was Jesus' miracle to me. That experience led me to a greater trust in the wisdom of the Church's teachings.
—*Donna Ulrich*

I love being Catholic because it means I never have to carry the weight of my struggles alone.
—*Claire Darnell*

Several years ago after Mass, I picked up a free book titled *Rediscover Jesus* and was also introduced to "Best Lent Ever," and that is when I began to fall in love with being Catholic. Since that time I have attended adult education classes at my church (something I would not have done in the past) and have learned about the saints, contemplative prayer, and the life of Jesus and what it means for us.
—*Amy Thompson-Aho*

I love being Catholic, because it's a challenge. I love a good challenge and striving to achieve new goals. My hobbies have always been things that are challenging: learning the piano, learning a new language, disciplining myself for a bodybuilding competition, even my profession is a challenge every day—and so is being Catholic.

Being Catholic is challenging, because Jesus calls us to perfection. He calls for us to discipline our selfish desires and put others before ourselves . . . and to put him first. And that's precisely what helps us grow in relationship with him.

Being Catholic is challenging, because in every generation we follow Jesus and go against the grain. In every generation, the current culture of the world wants us compromise on truth and love, but the Catholic Church never wavers. She maintains that we have been given the fullness of the faith from God Incarnate and we have no right to change that truth. The truth supersedes time and culture.

Being Catholic is challenging intellectually. We have a fascinating history of brilliant theologians, philosophers, and scientists. There is always more to learn—a lifetime is not long enough for our finite minds to grasp an infinite God. Which also means, we need to realize that there are limits to what we can understand. It's a challenge to recognize that there are limits to what we can understand and trust him even when it goes beyond human understanding.

Being Catholic is challenging because it requires us to look at our own lives and be honest with ourselves before we participate in the sacrament of reconciliation. A few years ago, I got to hear Matthew Kelly speak in person. He issued three options and challenged each of us to pick one to start doing:

1. Spend fifteen minutes each day reading the Gospels.
2. Use a *Mass Journal* to write down one point from Mass that speaks to you.
3. Start going to confession once a month.

Reconciliation was the one I wanted to do the least, which is why I chose that one: it's a challenge!
—*Don Sinak*

Growing up in the sixties with two Catholic parents, I knew at a very young age that my parents did not love each other very much. They often barely seemed to tolerate one another and had separate bedrooms. But being Catholic, they felt they had to stay together. I recall feeling awkward and caught in the middle when running interference for them ("Tell your father dinner is ready"; "Tell your mother I'm not hungry.") and trying to cope with the inescapable tension that resided in our small house. It wasn't very pleasant growing up in this volatile environment, and as I grew older, I found many reasons to excuse myself from the house. One of my favorite places to escape to was our local Catholic church, which was within walking distance. The peace I found there was a balm to my battered soul and one I often escaped to.

Matthew Kelly talks about the classroom of silence, and I think my love of silence started in those quiet moments sitting in the empty or almost-empty pews at church. I may have been too young to understand that I was laying my wounds and troubles at the feet of the Lord, but that is what I was doing, and he never failed to soothe me. I would enter overwhelmed and confused, but after sitting in the darkened, quiet church, I would leave in a much calmer frame of mind, able to cope once more. I have many happy memories of baptisms, confirmations, weddings, etc. as a Catholic, but will never forget God's warm embrace as I sat in the classroom of silence as a child.
—*Name Withheld*

I was not raised Catholic. My family wasn't religious in any real sense, although my mother told me stories about Jesus when I was young. Like many people in the sixties, I wasn't "into" any church, although I secretly believed in God and made up a lenient and convenient spiritual code to live by. Rudderless years flew by filled with excesses, abuses, divorces, and generally sin-filled behavior. My "code" flexed around all of that. Despite this, I was a successful person (by society's standards) whose bad behavior was routinely rewarded.

Over the years, in my heart, I knew I was hiding from the truth. The week of my fifty-eighth birthday, on an impulse, I drove over to my neighborhood church and attended my first Mass. I was so nervous, thoroughly convinced that everyone there could sense how inappropriate it was that I was there. After Mass, I stayed seated until most people had left, but as I stood to go, I was suddenly face to face with Father Cyril, who stretched out his hand and warmly welcomed me. I quickly explained that I was not Catholic, not anything really, and he touched my shoulder and told me not to worry because Jesus loved me anyway. He told me to come back. And I did. Over the next dozen Sundays, as I sat through each Mass, I felt like every homily was a personal message to me about how to right my ship. It wasn't easy—I had to own up to my many shortfalls—but I committed to becoming a Catholic then and there.

What I learned from Fr. Cyril was what I love most about being Catholic: God does love us, even those who resist it, and he invites us in and is ever prepared to show us how to become a-better-version-of-ourselves, even if we have denied him for decades.
—*Charles Shepard*

During 2009–2014, I had four foot surgeries and became addicted to opiate pain meds, which escalated into heroin. A stay-at-home mom who dropped her kids off at Holy Family School in her white Escalade, then headed straight to the projects to buy her dope. I would even pray a CD of the rosary on my way to pick up my drugs. Pretty screwed up, right?

Through three separate jails stints, two felonies, two separate rehabs and an *enormous* amount of pain and suffering that I caused myself and my precious family, I knew God was with me, but it was I who was filling my "God-sized hole" with something obviously other than God. When I was in my last rehab, I had the opportunity to go to confession. I was so nervous. I had committed so many sins throughout my addiction . . . was it really possible for God to forgive me through this priest? What if I forgot a sin I committed? I thought, *Well, at least I don't know this particular priest, that way I don't have to face him weekly!* I was fortunate this priest was extremely compassionate with me. I honestly felt my sins were washed away by the grace of God. How utterly amazing is *that!*

Now the "real" work had to begin: forgiving *myself.* How is it that God can forgive us, yet it is sooo hard forgiving ourselves? It's been quite a journey, and I'm humbled and grateful to say I have been clean for nearly three years, and my twenty-three-year marriage is stronger than it has ever been.
—*DeEtte Gastel*

I have found a home in the Catholic Church. I am a community-driven person and someone who needs accountability. The Catholic Church has provided me with a community that is more

like family—people who walk with me and encourage me to become the-best-version-of-myself in everything I do.
—*Katie Ferrara*

I love being Catholic because it gives meaning to everything I do. The Mass is filled with so much meaning—every word is said on purpose, for a reason, and the ritual of the Mass is something that has been done for so long. As a "cradle Catholic," I feel like I have learned so much in the last several years from the things Dynamic Catholic has put out there, things I wish I had been taught when I was little. Now that I have my own kids, it is so exciting to me to pass on to them the excitement I now have for the Catholic Church. My second-grade son and I have gone through the Blessed curriculum in addition to his regular CCD classes (they haven't implemented it yet at the parish), and he has changed his entire outlook on the Mass, the sacraments, and the Catholic faith. This has opened my eyes to how powerful it is for a young kid to have such a strong foundation to fall back on when things at school or with friends go wrong.
—*Abby Boley*

Whether life is going well or I'm having a rough patch, I *always* feel better after attending Mass. So many times, I hear exactly what I need to hear. There is a calming element of the Mass that helps me to refocus, reenergize, and remember why I love being Catholic.
—*Angie Gould-Wilmington*

I love being Catholic because of the miracles I experience because of my faith. I lost my husband in December very unexpectedly, and the only reason I'm making it day by day is because of my faith and knowing that this is God's plan and that my husband is in heaven watching over me and our children. I hear God telling me that it's okay, that he's got this, and to not be afraid.

—Emilie Lancour

I love being a Catholic because I can share in the Last Supper every day at Mass and imagine myself sitting with Jesus and his disciples, over and over. It never gets old or boring. There is always something new in this wonderful, awesome sacrament.

—Sandy Buttry

We were just on vacation this past week in Aruba and went to Mass. I thought it was so cool that the Mass in Aruba is the same Mass we experience at our home parish in Cedar Rapids, Iowa.

—Nick Rakers

I grew up Methodist, which gave me a good foundation, and to this day I have a deep love for the Bible. It was this foundation, along with personal struggles with my family life, that led me to seek more.

At one point I hit rock bottom. A friend invited me to her Catholic church, but then, for some reason, that Sunday she could not go. Consequently, I decided to go to another denomination's church not far away. When I got there, I discovered that this church had moved.

Determined to go to church somewhere, by God's grace I remembered the street where the Catholic church was located. As I walked down that street, I felt the arms of God pulling me lovingly. What came to mind was the Good Shepherd.

When I arrived at the church, I experienced the presence of God like never before. I knew without a doubt that he was there and that the Holy Spirit was surrounding me like a blanket. I experienced the Real Presence, without understanding the theology. I experienced Jesus both in the Mass and through the people. A lady invited me to sit with her. The music was led by the youth that Sunday. I was impressed that the Catholic Church was so open to young people.

After Mass, walking back to my college campus, two girls from that church pulled over and offered me a ride. They invited me to lunch with other young people. Such simple things, yet one of those girls started taking me to Mass on Sundays and to RCIA. When I returned to campus, I was completely overjoyed—never did I have such an experience at church.

My joy was so obvious that four of my friends came to Mass with me the next Sunday. The Lord continued to nurture me through RCIA, the kind people I met, the perpetual Adoration chapel at that parish, and also through a Catholicism class. On April 24, 2005, I entered the Church. The church's name is Sacred Heart, and I have a deep love for the Sacred Heart of Jesus. You can probably imagine why!

—*Catherine Clarke*

I love the beauty and simplicity of the Mass.
—*Ron Derr*

I love being Catholic because I always feel forgiven and loved. I never feel alone. I know Jesus and his Blessed Mother love me for myself. I know they never give up on me. I was a foster child abandoned by her parents, but I remember a nun telling me to just say aloud, "Hello, Jesus, this is Mary" whenever I felt sad or lonely. It worked then, and it still works now to help me focus on how loved I truly am.

—*Mary Starz*

At the core of my love for being Catholic is the Eucharist. When I receive the Eucharist, I receive Jesus, and I carry him out into the world with me. Wow!

—*Delia Kavanaugh*

One of the reasons I love being Catholic is our non-verbal prayers. I come from a Protestant background, and when I was first exposed to the Catholic faith, I was bewildered by all the Signs of the Cross, kneeling, standing, etc. It seemed like a bunch of meaningless voodoo, or traditional nonsense without added value.

But then I learned how Catholics enter the church buildings. As we enter the doorway to the church, we dip our fingers in the water and cross ourselves. Why? It is a non-verbal way to say "It is only by my baptism and Christ's death on the cross that I am worthy to enter into this place, and presence of God." That moment was a turning point for me. This was something I could get behind 100 percent, and it instantly transformed all the "voodoo" into deep, meaningful prayer and worship. It opened the door to a new way to love and honor God.

—*Alton Lee*

I'm thirty-five years old and have been Catholic and believed in God my whole life. However, in my younger years when I was in high school and early college, I remember thinking, *Well, there are so many religions that believe in God—Catholic, Protestant, Lutheran, Baptist—I wonder which one is the "right" one. Or are we all just going in the right direction because we believe in God?* It wasn't until I discovered Dynamic Catholic that I slowly but surely came to the realization, "Wow! I actually belong to the right one!"

There is so much truth in the saying "the genius of Catholicism." The minute I had that "aha!" moment, my faith deepened exponentially. The teachings that Jesus left behind for us in the Gospels are just that: genius!

I also love, as a mom to three beautiful little girls, being able to have solid answers for life's difficulties. I truly do not know how people survive without faith. I enjoy every single teachable moment I have with my children where I can say his name and reassure them because of him.

—*Michelle Hurley*

I have been attending the same Catholic church with my husband and three children for the last twelve years. It's a warm and welcoming church, the way I feel it should be.

When my mother died in 2014, I found myself struggling. I needed to live my life, but was afraid that I would have to "let her go" in order to move forward. My friend and co-worker saw that and gave me a copy of *Rediscover Catholicism*. It was so simple and made so much sense! It comforted me. My husband and I then attended a Passion and Purpose event, and that is where I became a Dynamic Catholic Ambassador.

Now for a confession: I am not Catholic. My husband is and our children are, but I struggle with taking that step. But I believe

in Catholicism! The Catholic Church seems to be the only church that stays true to its teachings and is not swayed by the times. I know it has flaws, but what doesn't?
—*Andrea Tamburri*

I love being Catholic because of the unity that love for the Eucharist brings about, along with devotion to the Blessed Mother.
—*Fr. Shaun Foggo*

I love being a Catholic. It is the one constant part of my life.
—*Marie Edlund*

Being Catholic you have the opportunity to go to Mass and receive the Eucharist not just once a week but every day! Since I retired almost five years ago, I've tried to make daily Mass a part of my life. I think it has changed me in many ways. First of all I feel more aware of God's presence in my life. Secondly, I want to reach out and help people more often. It also helps me to be more patient with my husband, who retired the year after I did. That I'm still working on!
—*Jeanne Riehs*

Two words: Holy Eucharist. Today I brought the Eucharist to a woman at a senior living facility who skipped lunch so she could receive. When I showed up in her room, tears came down her cheeks. She was so appreciative. The Catholic Church has what other churches simply do not have. What a gift—what a blessing.
—*Mark Rudloff*

I love being Catholic since it is my "home" on this earth for this short life. Early in life I realized that you had to live by something as your guide, and I felt that even if the whole Jesus thing was not true, to live by his teaching would result in the best society possible. But as I have aged I see that the scrutiny our faith has undergone just polishes the truth it proclaims and radiates to the world. I love the simplicity and complexity of this faith. It moves the simple, and yet it is complex enough that the learned can study it a lifetime without running out of amazing revelations and discoveries.
—*Carla Dill*

I love being Catholic because I love knowing that holiness is possible for me.
—*Natalie Gunawan*

I love being Catholic because I am part of a worldwide family. It doesn't matter what country or city I am in. When I go to Mass, I am home. This summer, for the first time, I visited several Baptist churches with my mother-in-law who was trying to find a new church when we all moved. She struggled to find one that was like her old church, but I was home just by celebrating the Mass with my Catholic family.
—*Mary Beth Lassiter*

There is a sense of pride and responsibility that comes with being Catholic. When I tell someone, "I'm Catholic," I tend to stand a little taller. Not because I think "I'm so much better than you," but because I feel like I am truly proud to be a part of the Church and everything it stands for. I feel like it is a great honor and privilege

and something I'm not ever ashamed of admitting. Jesus himself started the Catholic Church, and to be a part of that same community comes with a great deal of responsibility, honor, and pride.
—*Blayne Magdefrau*

Many people say the Catholic faith is stifling, harsh, and repressive. However, my experience with Catholicism has been hugely liberating, a faith truly based on encouraging and inspiring individualized thought and compassion.

For me, my Catholicism has been my biggest saving grace in all of my toughest times; it's been the most consistent, nurturing path I have found. The more I learn about the Catholic faith, the more I really appreciate my roots in it. I remain grateful that the seeds that were planted when I was a child blossomed when my life was in a negative tailspin.
—*Name Withheld*

Catholicism offers so many ways for laypeople to be the hands and feet of Jesus, therefore being a bright light attracting others to Jesus and our faith. There truly is something for everyone!
—*Andria Faust*

I am a convert to the faith. I grew up with many occult practices around me. I was lost. I was wandering through all the things that the world said would bring me happiness, but the search only made me emptier. As I learned more and more about the Catholic faith, I found solid ground: no more shifting sand. I found a true vision for the human person, an answer to the relativism our culture promotes. The truth set me free.
—*Kirsten Simonsgaard*

I've dealt with a lot of hard times over the last three years—loss in my family, anxiety, and health issues that have had me fighting for answers and hope. During this time more than ever before, I have pursued my Catholic faith. I never understood what being strong in my faith was until circumstances left me running fully into God's open arms in times of fear, anxiety, and frustration. As a result, I find hope. I find meaning. I find purpose.

—*Becky Church*

For those of us lucky enough to experience Catholicism as a way of life, life is overflowing with blessings. In keeping a spiritual journal, one in which I record experiences that I deem to be worthy of recording, it amazes me to discover over time that the most meaningful experiences of my life are now written to be enjoyed, learned from, and shared with family and friends forever.

—*Daryl Gonyon*

I love how I feel like I'm at home when I'm in the Catholic Church. It could be the worst week, there could be so much going on in my life, but when I enter those doors and sit down in the pew, nothing else really matters other than what's going on right there in front of me. Going to Mass really puts my life in perspective and sets my attitude for the week.

—*Jorge Suarez*

I was raised in a non-Christian home. My mother was anti-Christian. Somehow, though, I always knew Jesus loved me. When I was nine years old I told my mother she may not need God but I did. She told me I would grow out of this fairy tale. After getting married and having two children, I decided it was time to become Catholic. What I love most about the Church is that the priest accepted us with open arms even though my first child was born out of wedlock.

—*Jeanne Bullock*

Becoming Catholic is the best thing that has ever happened to me, and I don't mean that lightly. I started out as an atheist. For over twenty-three years I firmly believed that there was no God due to my difficult childhood and depression. I made a solemn vow to myself that I wasn't ever going to be pulled into the whole "believing in God" joke. I firmly believed that all Christians, and Catholics especially, were all just a bunch of do-gooders who thought they were better than everyone else.

My best friend (who also happens to be my cousin) is the one who knocked the sense into me. Let me tell you, we had some arguments, but once I understood the meaning of Catholicism and what it was all about, I wanted in! I figured, if I'm going to do this thing, I'm going to do it all! I wanted everything that God and Jesus had to offer, and I didn't want to do it lightly. If Jesus could give up his very life for me, the least I could do is believe in him and accept not some but *all* of his gifts and never take them for granted. That's why I'm Catholic, and despite what any critics say, I am proud of my faith!

—*Monique Billington*

I love being Catholic because of the long history and tradition. I feel safe with my Catholic faith; it is a well-worn, much-loved quilt handed down through many, many generations.

—*Peggy Tallon*

I love being Catholic because of the people. I'm overwhelmed by the caliber of people in my parish. Seeing others live out the Catholic faith is inspiring and pushes me to become the-best-version-of-myself.

—*Dave Carlton*

I am a cradle Catholic, but in my teens until my late twenties, I followed the three philosophies Matthew Kelly identified in one of his books: individualism, hedonism, and minimalism (in terms of my spiritual life). After some personal pain—my wife left me, my eldest son died in a motorcycle accident, and my youngest son turned to heroine to cope with life—I was blessed by encounters with Mother Teresa, Fr. Donald Calloway, and two great spiritual counselors who are also great friends. With all of this I have learned about the brilliance of Catholicism. Once I opened my heart to God, I wanted his truth to become part of me. It is a truth that I work at each day in spite of my weaknesses.

—*Tom Drapeau*

There are so many things I love about being Catholic—the Church's rich history of evangelization (especially the early Church), and the contributions to the arts and music, to social services, to healthcare and education. In every area in which people are in need, the Church has responded to those needs. I love that the Church is not afraid to go against the tide of secular society, to stay true to the Gospel. The older I get, the more I fall in love with my Catholic faith.

—*Therese DeSitter*

I love being Catholic because the Church has a strong intellectual tradition. For me, the motto of St. Anselm (1033–1109)—"faith seeking understanding"—means that we continually probe the ineffable mystery of God with reason. The Church reveres philosophy as the bridge between reason and faith. I have been educated and made my living as a scientist, and I am thankful that modern experimental science had its origin in the Catholic universities of Europe during the Middle Ages and the Renaissance.
—*Deacon Thomas J. Giacobbe*

St. Augustine said, "To fall in love with God is the greatest romance; to seek him, the greatest adventure; to find him, the greatest human achievement." Catholicism calls each of us into a romantic adventure with the Lord. Through the Church, God extends his mighty hand, inviting us to an authentic, love-until-it-hurts, soul-transcending, eternal romance.

I have been romanced by our heavenly Father at the foot of the cross, transformed in the heart of his Church. Though raised Catholic, it was only at the cross of a dark physical trial that his love-light broke through. In the aftermath of sudden illness, job loss, and poorly coping with all I had become, I fell on the rocky soil of my soul. There, crushed beneath the weight of my cross, he met me with the unfathomable light of his merciful love.

In a myriad of intimate encounters, he loved me amid the raw pain of my brokenness. He held a mirror up to my soul, called me to repentance, and enveloped me in his merciful embrace. His love and light broke into the darkest suffering of my life. He resurrected my Catholic faith and graced me with unshakable peace and joy. My divine physician healed me in ways I didn't even know I needed. He pursued me relentlessly. He called me back to life. This is the beauty of the Catholic faith. It understands that with life's blessings there is inevitable suffering from the fallen nature of humanity. Yet there is hope for all the faithful during every season of life. As St. John Paul II said, "We are the Easter people and hallelujah is our song."

—*Katie McGaver*

Every Sunday, after being fed by the Word of God, my husband and I join our faith community and eagerly approach the altar for Holy Communion. Returning to our seats, we kneel in prayer as we watch our brothers and sisters in Christ reach out their hands to receive our Lord. Old and young, singles and families—we are all one body through Christ who strengthens us.

One particular Sunday, we were privileged to witness a beautiful portrait of love, commitment, and hope. A young mother, struggling but determined, processed forward with her disabled, eleven-year-old daughter. Not wanting to maneuver the cumbersome wheelchair through the worship space, this faithful mother, who was not much larger than her daughter, carried her child to the altar. Without hesitation, she carried her. Hopeful despite all limitations, she raised her daughter up to receive her Lord and Savior. My husband and I were awestruck.

That single moment in time has often led us to reflect particularly on our commitment as husband and wife. When we are faced with weakness, hardship, or discouragement, our bond is tested. Sometimes it's hard to carry one another through the difficult times—to raise one another up so that we see the image of Christ disguised by our brokenness. But that's exactly where he meets us and delivers us—in and through brokenness. So we process forward in a loving communion that draws us to the life-giving

Communion. The witness and support of other faithful husbands and wives encourage us along the way. Through their example and prayers, we can raise one another up, despite our weaknesses, and receive all that the Lord desires to share with us. This is the blessing of the sacraments. This is what I love about being Catholic.

—*Ann Mauro-Vetter*

My journey has been an interesting one, to say the least. During the seventies, I was sort of a hippie and somewhat rebellious, especially toward my father. I was in Catholic high school at the time and didn't have a personal relationship with Jesus Christ. It was crazy, but my sister entered a convent, and about six months later, my dad told me to go and visit her in Boston. While there, at first I joked and made fun of the nuns a little, and I never thought I could give my life to God like my sister did.

A couple days later, I got sick and ended up in bed. The mother superior offered me a book to read called *Heaven*, written by the founder of that religious order. I read it and decided to stay there for four years and three months because I wanted to know God and have a personal relationship with him like all the sisters did; they seemed so joyful and at peace.

Looking back, I realized that God laid the foundation for me by talking to me through that book. I'm so grateful I went to visit my sister in Boston. All the experiences I had at the convent drew me closer and closer to God and prepared me to face the world today.

I'm proud to be called Catholic because of its reasonable truths and its beauty, and that beauty is Jesus Christ who wants my total happiness and wants me to be with him in heaven!

—*Therese Tamburello*

I love being Catholic now more than ever since coming back to the Church five years ago. I also love my *Mass Journal*, which I have kept for over four years, thanks to Matthew Kelly.

—*Hector Zayas*

I love being Catholic because God placed this love in my heart from a very early age. My family was Catholic. I was baptized, but when I was four, my family left the Church. A young priest had come to our parish, bringing Vatican II, and my family did not approve. I missed going to church so much and would ask them if we could go back. They said no. Even though I was raised with no faith, there was something about being Catholic that called to me. As an adult, I tried out other churches, but no other church felt like "home."

Two years ago, I felt the tug to come home. I knew I needed to start with confession. While talking to the priest and telling him the story of my family leaving due to Vatican II, he recalled when some of his parishioners left the Church for the same reason.

He asked where I grew up. I told him. He asked me the name of my parish. I told him.

He gently reached over and said, "My dear, I was the young priest that brought Vatican II to your family's church all those years ago. You are supposed to be here. You've come full circle." As an interesting side note, he retired a month later.

—*Kathleen Zelnik*

My husband and I talk all the time about how our society seems to have a "malaise" over it. Nothing seems to be a big deal anymore. The way we dress, speak, act—nothing about it seems sacred or of

any importance, but Jesus uses Catholicism to make everything a big deal. He uses a simple rooster's crow in the Passion to signify to Peter his denial, he uses all we take for granted and makes it a big deal. Life is a big deal, and Catholicism reminds me through the Mass, prayers, and silence, that all of life is sacred; it makes it a big deal again. Without these reminders, I too would quickly and easily fall into the same trap. Catholicism grounds me.
—*Tina Waechter*

I love the holistic opportunity Jesus presents to us in his life and in his ministry! Living a holistic, joyful, and authentic Catholic lifestyle is such an incredible way to live. I love that there are no coincidences and God can find purpose in anything. Having a personal relationship with Jesus as the foundation of your life is the most peaceful and foundational part of thriving in life, not just surviving.
—*William Rein*

I've often heard the saying the Catholic Church has the fullness of truth, but I actually experienced this in a very personal way when my sixteen-year-old special-needs son died in 2016. I love being Catholic because without the love, mercy, and beauty of our faith I would have been lost at the death of my beloved son. Instead, I have hope that one day we will be together again, but until then I have this beautiful Church to guide me.
—*Jennifer Colsch*

I love being Catholic, because it is where God called me. I was not raised in any faith—my parents called themselves non-denominational Protestants. We did not go to church. I heard about God and Jesus, but I knew nothing about them. After I married my Catholic husband, I started to go to Mass with him and my daughter, because I had heard that the family that prays together stays together. One day at Mass I felt this incredible blanket of love enfold me. I had never felt anything that strong. It was warm and unconditional and directed at me. Everything in the church faded as I basked in this love.

I eventually realized, as my husband and daughter would go up to receive Holy Communion, that the love was coming from the Host. It was at that time I knew I wanted to become Catholic and be a part of what was in the Church. My most memorable moment as a Catholic was the day I became Catholic in 1986 at the age of thirty-six. It was the beginning of a new life for me. I truly felt reborn, and this exciting, fulfilling journey has never ended.
—*Anne Dunn*

I love being a Catholic because I feel I am home. I am the only Catholic in my family. My parents called themselves Christians, but I have very few memories of them taking us to church when I was a child. What I do remember is them wanting Sunday mornings to themselves, so my sister and I attended whatever local church would pick us up on the bus. Since I moved around a lot as a child, I got to experience a variety of churches, including non-denominational, Methodist, Southern Baptist, and Calvary Chapel. I felt called to Jesus, but in all of these churches there was always something missing. The first time I attended a Catholic Mass, I found it. I can't explain what the feeling was except to say "home."
—*Crystal Martinez*

Two

What Is Your Favorite Memory as a Catholic?

My favorite memory is rediscovering my faith after a twenty-year departure by going on retreat and making my first confession since I was ten years old. I've been able to gradually leverage that magnificent moment of feeling God's mercy into a plan of life that includes daily Mass, morning and evening prayer, daily rosaries, spiritual reading, weekly confession, spiritual direction, annual retreats, and more in the twenty-five years since.
—*Patrick Ciriacks*

My favorite memory is attending a Catholic Marriage Encounter Weekend retreat with my estranged husband. It is a long story of hurt and pain that separated us and pulled us apart and had us living in separate locations. He was living in an apartment, and I was living in our home with our two children, hoping for but doubting that a miracle would occur to save my sweet, young little family.

Prayer is powerful, and handing your problems over to God is powerful. I'm not sure how God saved us; there were so many teeth in the wheels that had to line up in order for every event to coordinate and work out. But I do know that this Marriage Encounter Weekend and the people presenting there helped save our marriage. I saw the love the presenting couples had for each other, and I wanted what they had. Our problems were bigger than a Marriage Encounter Weekend could presume to help with, and we were encouraged to attend a Retrouvaille Weekend. We planned on finding one, but with our continued support from Marriage Encounter and attending monthly "Love Circle" meetings with our Marriage Encounter group, we continued to heal and grow close together again.

That was twenty-six years ago, and we've been married for thirty-four years this coming August. We are both proud of our marriage, and we both know we never want to go down that road again. Our problems made us grow closer together and closer to God.

—*Ruth Ann Reed*

My favorite memories are yet to come; my closest and most meaningful relationships center around gathering in the Church.

—*Paula Curry*

My favorite memory is learning about prayer . . . I am a happier, kinder person because of what I've learned about prayer through the Catholic Church.

—*Jim Hoffman*

I am a cradle Catholic who fell away from regularly practicing my faith in my mid-twenties, and only recently (about four years ago), found myself in a personal crisis, just having gone through a second divorce. I am sixty-nine years old and was married twenty-five years the first time and twenty years the second. Without going through all the details of those years, some wonderful, some turbulent, I found myself, four years ago, on my knees in the nearest Catholic church, soul-searching and praying to our Lord for help, for guidance, for his presence in my life. On my way out of the church, there was a book sitting on the table in the gathering space. I picked it up, began reading, and could not put it down. I took the book to the parish office to ask if I could purchase it, and the secretary told me that Father had purchased one for everyone in the parish. I told her it was the last one. She said, "It must be yours." That book was *Rediscovering Catholicism*. It was the beginning of my journey back, and the profound realization that God has been with me all along. Each "next" step I took, there appeared the right person or right book, or right experience that not only brought me back, but transformed my life. I still struggle at times, but I struggle with confidence that God is there ALWAYS, and I trust in him.

—*Joyce Porritt*

A long time ago, when my non-Catholic future husband and I were dating, he invited me to attend his church. I did, after going to Mass at my church. Everyone (literally) welcomed me and invited me to various functions. The pastor made a point of talking with me and finding out a bit about me. I left feeling as though I'd just been adopted. At home, I thought about the experience, and listened to the little voice that asked, "What will you do if this becomes the deal breaker? What if he asks you to leave your church?"

I'd been Catholic all my life. School with the nuns, learning my *Catechism* lessons, being part of the choir, retreats, novenas to Our

Lady, receiving Communion—I loved it all. What convinced me, though, was that if I left my church, I couldn't receive our Lord. And any children we had would be raised in a non-Catholic church.

Understand, I deeply loved this man. I would have done almost anything to keep him in my life, but I could never leave my church. I could never not be Catholic.

My passion for my faith must have made an impression. He began going to Mass with me, and he became Catholic before we were married.

—*Carol Brodtrick*

My favorite memory as a Catholic is Sister Mary Dennis, our seventh grade religion teacher. She was old, strict, and demanding, but everyone loved her! Sr. Dennis was from a large Catholic family in Chicago, and she loved to tell us stories about growing up in that family. She had a disabled sister who was mostly confined to bed, and that sister was the real inspiration to several of her siblings who were priests or nuns.

At our Catholic elementary school, we attended daily morning Mass. But that wasn't good enough for Sr. Dennis. She challenged us to also attend Mass on Saturday mornings—which meant getting up early and walking to church. "You mean daily weekday Mass plus Sunday isn't enough? We have to go all seven days?" Yep! She also challenged us to go into church after school or during recess whenever possible to do the Stations of the Cross on our own. So we did. Both! On any given Saturday morning the church would have a group of Sr. Dennis' seventh grade class in attendance. And many also stayed for the Stations. Of course, after that we would meet at the soda fountain across the street for "fellowship" and breakfast. We each had to keep a chart of our attendance to encourage discipline. Over the years, this practice taught me that the "optional" events at church were actually some of the most spiritual and moving of all. I loved the evening devotions to the Blessed Virgin Mary in October, special feast day celebrations, and Adoration of the Blessed Sacrament. I don't know if I would ever have participated in the extras without the challenges and heartfelt encouragement from Sr. Mary Dennis!

—*Ann Molteni Bridenstine*

I was born in India in 1953 to a devout, God-fearing Catholic family. My dad was an exemplary Catholic, a university professor who wore his faith on his sleeves. He came from a village whose Catholic faith goes back to the time of St. Francis Xavier in the sixteenth century. We were the only Christian family in the neighborhood. We were surrounded by people of every other religious tradition: Hindu, Muslim, Buddhist, etc. We stood out because of the way we lived our faith.

My dad was a daily communicant. He rose every morning at 4:30 a.m., whether it was January or June. He would go in silence to the church, which was about a twenty-five-minute walk from home. I recall one of our neighbors, a devout Brahmin attorney, telling others, "If you want to see Jesus, look out of your window at 5:00 a.m. and you will see him walking down the street."

After Mass, my dad would remain in Adoration for twenty minutes. On reaching home, he would take his New Testament and *The Imitation of Christ* to spend a half-hour meditation, to model himself on Christ. Then he would drink his coffee and read the daily newspaper, eat his breakfast, and get ready to go to the university.

—*Dr. Robert Berchmans, PhD*

I remember preparing for my confirmation, which occurred while my family was living in Italy. I had been attending classes in preparation for the big event, and I was ready and very excited to receive the gift of the Holy Spirit. It was a big old church with beautiful surrounding gardens. I had a simple but elegant dress and killer Italian strappy shoes—I felt very grown up. As the priest anointed me with oil and made the Sign of the Cross on my forehead, I literally felt a burning in my throat. I thought I needed water at the time, but I know now it was the true and real gift of the Holy Spirit entering into me, and it lives within me to this day.

—*Siobhan Peryer*

On Saturday, March 12, 2011, I was rescued by the Wayne County Search and Rescue after spending six days stranded in No Man's Canyon in southeastern Utah. My confinement was the result of a climbing accident that had claimed the life of my brother Louis. I had no way to go down or out the way we hiked in. I'd left a map behind of our hiking plans, and our loved ones expected us to call on Thursday during our return trip home. Without any word from us, our family called the authorities, and a search and rescue effort began.

I spent most of those 144 hours on a three-by-twelve sandstone ledge in a desolate and narrow slot section of the canyon. I prayed the Our Father and recited the Hail Mary frequently. Soon after my rescue, I was airlifted by helicopter to Moab Regional Hospital, where I received emergency care for dehydration and malnutrition.

But what I needed more than medical attention was spiritual attention. I asked the attending doctor if there was a priest on duty in the hospital. To my dismay, there wasn't, but the doctor assured me he'd check into my request further.

When Dr. Steven Houzer returned later, he boosted my mood with the news that if a priest wasn't available in the hospital, he'd take me to meet one. After I showered and changed into borrowed clothes from his friend, Captain Tim Peoples, we drove to Saturday evening Mass at Pius X Catholic Church.

It was the first Sunday in Lent. The Gospel reading was the story of Jesus and his forty days in the wilderness. *I'd come out of my trial in the wilderness hours before.*

While my life had been saved and I'd soon would be united with loved ones, what I needed most was to be united with Christ: first, in the Eucharist and then in a private conversation with Father Bill Wheaton after Mass.

In the sanctuary, I wept and unburdened myself to Fr. Wheaton, expressing my anguish and guilt over losing my brother. Excusing himself momentarily, he returned to comfort me with the sacrament of healing, the anointing of the sick. *Fr. Wheaton knew what I needed most in that moment.*

The journey of my healing had begun.

—*David Cicotello*

I was born in Wiesbaden, Germany, on January 13, 1939. In September 1939, World War II broke out. Under Adolf Hitler's regime, any religion, including Roman Catholicism, was severely suppressed. My mother, Berta Schmalstieg, supported the two of us as a teacher (my father was never in the picture) and consequently had to follow Hitler's rules and was not a practicing Catholic. Therefore, I did not get baptized as a baby. After the war ended and after her three-month imprisonment, a close friend of my mother's, Annie Möller, convinced her to have me baptized. Yes, those times were wild and rough. We were very poor as we had no income. We were hungry at times, and we even went begging. My mom explained to me: "This life is a big adventure."

My mother and Annie made arrangements for my baptism at the Monastery and Pilgrimage Church Maria Martental, which presumably was founded by a convent according to the Rule of St. Augustine in 1145. Today it belongs to the Carmelites. During the war, from 1941 to 1945, the monastery and pilgrimage chapel Maria Martental were misappropriated to the Hitler Youth. After the war priests dedicated to the Heart of Jesus took over and constructed the monastery again. The chapel was still in fairly good condition.

Thus, on October 10, 1945, I was baptized. I still remember the details. It started out with a four-mile hike. The chapel was very dark, yet to me it was comforting and secure. The holy water fountain was in front of a *pietà* sculpture.

During and after the baptism, I had the feeling that Jesus and his mother were welcoming me into their family, and this brought me love and joy. I felt happy, protected, and safe. Afterward we celebrated in front of the Pilgrimage Chapel, sitting on old, partially torn, wooden benches and eating a picnic lunch Annie had prepared. It was a wonderful experience, and today I still love the *pietà* prayer: *Drück die Wunden, die Dein Sohn für mich empfunden tief in meine Seele ein* (Press the wounds your Son suffered for me deeply into my soul).

—*Helga Ingeborg Howard*

How I became a Catholic is a treasured memory that began when I bought a bingo ticket from a nun. How Catholic is that?

Back in the early eighties, I was a non-practicing, non-participating in any formal religion Protestant. My husband, Mike, was a non-practicing Catholic. Our first home was on a quiet street in the suburbs of Pittsburgh, and our neighbors were the Sisters of the Holy Spirit.

The bingo ticket transaction led me to the stairs at the front entrance of the Motherhouse of the Sisters of the Holy Spirit. I had no idea that climbing those stairs was the beginning of my faith journey as a Catholic. Silly me, I thought I was going to pay for the bingo ticket I'd purchased from a nun earlier in the week.

Sister Damien met me with a smile and a gracious welcome. After we took care of business, she guided me into the chapel, where my senses were treated to an unexpected banquet. The stillness was palpable; the sweet scent of incense lingered in the air, and my gaze became affixed to the stunningly beautiful mosaic of the Holy Spirit on the east wall.

The deep peace I felt in that moment is a memory I will have forever. I was in God's house, and it felt good to be there.

Sr. Damien invited me to Mass the next day. I went, and Mike came with me. After we attended for the next few Sundays, I grew curious and noticed that along with the peace I had been feeling, there was a new energy in my heart. I asked Sr. Damien how I could learn more about Catholicism and becoming a Catholic. She told me to call their chaplain, the priest who celebrated Mass in their chapel. At the time he was Bishop Anthony G. Bosco, auxiliary bishop of the Diocese of Pittsburgh.

After just a few moments on the phone with Bishop Bosco, he established that Mike and I were the ones who were "sitting in the back of the bus"—a.k.a., the last pew—for the last few weeks, and that *maybe* God had "nudged" me with the bingo ticket and the tour of the chapel.

I wondered. Was it a "nudge"?

We scheduled an appointment to meet. During our meeting Bishop Bosco told me he would like to instruct me in the faith. I liked that idea. We made a plan to meet weekly. Even with his very full schedule, he made time to meet with me most every week for a year.

As I was introduced to and learned about the magisterium of the Church, grew in the faith, and was received into the Catholic Church, some very special graces were manifesting. The bishop and the sisters became friends, not only with me, but with Mike as well. He was beside me on this journey and came back into the Church.

I will be forever grateful for the Sisters of the Holy Spirit, the "nudge," and that my teacher, my guide on this journey, was one of God's most brilliant, generous, and faithful servants—a true disciple.

—*Jan McCarthy*

My favorite memory is of the moment that I truly claimed the Catholic faith as my own. I had been raised Catholic in a practicing home, become a non-practicing "spiritual person" during college, and returned to regular participation in a warm and welcoming Protestant church during my mid-twenties. That church was instrumental in bringing me back to worship, but still in a short time I had begun to feel a longing for the richness and fullness of the church I'd known as a child.

One day I decided to visit my former parish; there was no service at the time, so the church was quiet. I stepped into a pew and knelt down. I remember so clearly the fragrance of incense and warm candle wax, the feel of the kneeler beneath me as I leaned forward to the warmly worn pew in front of me, the sight of my beautiful Blessed Mother welcoming me. In that moment all of my senses gathered the church around me like an embrace, and I knew I was home.

—*Pamela Kavanaugh*

A favorite Catholic memory was made just this past Easter Sunday, April 1, 2018. I was at my home parish, and like all Catholic churches on an Easter Sunday, it was adorned with beautiful flowers. Joyful music celebrating the resurrection of Jesus filled the sanctuary. Parishioners and their out-of-town guests filled the pews. Mass proceeded as usual until a toddler, a little escapee from one of the pews, walked down the center aisle of the church and took up a position in front of the altar. He stood there watching Father Jim prepare for the Liturgy of the Eucharist.

There was almost an audible sigh from the congregation. We were in a grace-filled moment.

When the child caught Fr. Jim's eye, our pastor gave him a smile, and I think I saw him wink at the little one.

The toddler's dad calmly walked to the front of the church to retrieve his son. Gently taking him by the hand, they returned to their pew and Mass continued. But it wasn't the same. I had a renewed awareness of what was taking place.

What a wonderful gift this little one gave to all of us when he drew close to the altar to see what was happening. We should all, old and young, want to draw close to Christ as did this little escapee from the pew. "And a little child shall lead them" (Isaiah 11:6).

—*Nancy Bricker*

Ten years ago, I was a postulant in a religious community in New Jersey. Several sisters, including those of us in formation, had the privilege of attending an ordination for a priest. That is easily the most extraordinary ceremony I've attended, except for perhaps my own wedding. I felt the Holy Spirit's presence in such a profound way that I cried throughout the whole Mass. I may never have the privilege of attending an ordination again, but it is something I will forever carry in my heart and soul. It is an event I wish every Catholic could attend.

—*July Sanchez-Sadowski*

As a high school theology teacher I have many great memories on retreats and trips with my students. One of the things they love to do is pray in Adoration with worship music every Thursday night. Last Thanksgiving we had a lot of alumni come back for it and had about one hundred high-school and college students praying, reading, singing, and crying. It's always very powerful to see that, and I wish other people saw that side of the Church that is young, prayerful, and full of enthusiasm!

—*Dan Finocchio*

My favorite memory as a Catholic was growing in my faith as a teenager. My awakening in my faith began in the summer of 1984. I was so blessed to meet two amazing people that impacted my life and left an impression on me to this very day. A priest named Father Donald Henry and a nun named Sister Judy Baldino came to my parish. I was thirteen, shy, and naïve, and just went to church because that was what was expected. I don't remember getting anything from it. Church felt cold and stale. I knew it was the right thing to do to go to church on the weekend, but it did not inspire me. I didn't know how my faith was to fit into my life all the other days of the week.

My past experiences with parish priests were stern and routine. I will never forget the first time I met Fr. Henry. He was a blonde-haired, blue-eyed, smiling-from-ear-to-ear priest dressed in a T-shirt and shorts. That smile never seemed to leave his face. Oddly, I found myself smiling back. He was very talented at engaging and inspiring people. He brought out the best in people.

A few days later I met Sr. Judy, who was to be our pastoral assistant. I was intrigued as I never knew a woman to have such a position in the parish. Sr. Judy was Italian to the core, with an energetic personality, and loved to sing. I loved to sing, but I was very shy about it. These two people had something attractive about them, and I could not get enough of being around them. Little did I know that these two individuals would influence me to become who I am today. I began to explore my faith with their encouragement.

Sr. Judy picked up on my love of singing and took this shy girl and stretched her confidence enough to convince her to sing in the new choir she'd formed. Today, I sing as a cantor at church, and I do weddings and funerals. My singing has become a second form of prayer that I offer for others.

Fr. Henry was a great homilist. I would often leave church with something from his homily that sparked my curiosity to learn more about my faith. He was on fire for Christ and the Church. It was so attractive. I learned through him that giving of my time and talents was very important work to do. It was in that work that I discovered my love and talent for teaching. And I had an ability to connect with children with disabilities. I found myself drawn to help them, and in turn I grew better every day as a person.

I had over nine years of their influence in my life. I began to form a daily prayer life with their guidance. I am eternally grateful for Fr. Henry and Sr. Judy. I was so blessed as a teenager to meet them. It changed the course of my life for the better. It was God's plan to bring them into my life as a teenager.

Today, I teach Decision Point to the eighth graders at my parish. Over sixty candidates have gone through the program since we started it in 2014. I work with three other adult instructors and our parish priest to make the program happen. We also have two former confirmation candidates that help with the program as well. We are making a difference. I am passing on what I have learned to others. Our faith is changing lives for the better.

—*Tina Seiger*

One time I was between jobs and in Mass, perhaps feeling more broken and helpless than the situation warranted. As the offering basket approached in the pews in front of me, I started debating with myself what to do. Widow's mite, widow's shmite, money was tight. As the basket came to me, impulsively I reached in my pocket and threw in everything I had. As I watched it bob down the pew, like an empty beer can floating around the rocks in a country creek, I thought, "I wonder how much money I gave."

After that moment, my life changed. An outlook that had seemed barren and bleak became plentiful. Within a few weeks I was interviewing for five different jobs—at the same time. Not knowing what to do, I decided to leave that to prayer and promised God I would give 10 percent to the Church (well, God had done a pretty good job to that point!).

I now recommend to everyone, believer or not, that they should anonymously give 10 percent of their after-tax income to charity. It changes you, and God is not the only one who will notice the change. I've never met anyone who gives 10 percent and does not become richer for it.

—*Eric Karl*

I have a story about getting my son home for Christmas. He had tickets, but on December 23 his boss kept him late at work although he had permission to leave early. He got a taxi (in Manhattan) two hours before his flight time. After being in the cab for an hour he sent a text to ask if I could find him another reservation because he was just sitting in traffic and thought he would miss his flight. My husband still had "status" with an airline, so I told him, and he got on the phone. Meanwhile I texted my son back and said that I would pray, and his answer was that he was already praying.

Now, a friend of mine was dying from a brain tumor, and she had been asking us to pray the Memorare, her favorite prayer, and I had been praying it multiple times a day. So I decided to pray that to help get my son home. However, at one point at the end of the prayer I just said, "Mary, I know that there is nothing that I need; I have a house, food, and shelter and in the great scheme of things I have everything, but if there is any way that you could help get my son home so that we can celebrate your son's birthday, I would really appreciate it."

Fifteen minutes before his flight was due to depart, my son texted me to say, "On plane, will tell you about it when I get home." We learned that thirty minutes before his flight, he was still in the cab. Suddenly his taxi changed lanes, there was no traffic, and the driver floored it. Our son arrived at the airport without his boarding pass and saw three kiosks. Two had lines and

the third was empty. Our son figured he had nothing to lose, put in his card, and out came the boarding pass. He ran to security, and the TSA agent was just closing it up but waved him through. He ran to the gate, and they had not yet given away his seat. . . . My son says it was a miracle, and I say it was the Mom Network!
—*Molly Sequeira*

My favorite memory is my present-day prayer time every morning for forty-five to sixty minutes as soon as I get my coffee. Being with God and drinking hot coffee is just a perfect way for me to face the day and trust that "all will be well."
—*Peggy Daniels*

I am sixty-two years old, and I grew up Catholic and have always been a "Catholic." I basically just went through the motions without truly understanding what I was doing until I read *Rediscover Catholicism*. In my case, the book could have been titled *DISCOVER Catholicism*. It literally changed my life, especially when I also read *The Rhythm of Life* and *Perfectly Yourself*. What is my favorite memory of being a Catholic? I am currently living it.
—*Barth Guillette*

My most recent memory was welcoming my daughter-in-law into the Catholic Church. It was driven by the Holy Spirit. It started three years ago on Christmas Eve. At the time she and my son were dating and expecting their first child. Things were not stable. They didn't show up for Christmas Eve Mass with the rest of the family. I worried that something was wrong and was afraid of what news I might get. Neither one of them would answer my text messages or calls.

They showed up at my sister's home for dinner and told me they just couldn't get it together and were sorry they missed Mass. My son asked me if I would take them to midnight Mass, and I agreed. Fr. Tom made an announcement at the end of Mass that they were going to open their doors for anyone who was thinking about becoming Catholic. As we walked out of church, my daughter-in-law said to me, "I would like to go to that meeting. I want to be Catholic."

She called me the day before the meeting and asked me if I was still willing to go with her. I said yes again. I picked her up, and on the way over she started to have second thoughts. She was embarrassed about being pregnant and not married. She said they would never let her in, that she was a sinner and a failure. I told her it would be all right and we wanted her to be part of our church. I told her the Holy Spirit touched her on Christmas Eve and she needed to let him lead her.

When we walked in, Fr. Tom was standing off to the side. We walked up to him and I introduced Jolie to him. I explained her situation and how she felt, and he said not to worry. He said, "We all have issues, and we would really like her to be part of our church." He took her aside and they talked for a few minutes. She came back with a smile and jumped in head first. Her journey took three years to accomplish. There were a lot of ups and downs, but she, on her own, stuck with it and was baptized this Easter at the Easter Vigil. It was amazing.

—*Tim Arnold*

I am a mom of four children, ages thirteen to twenty. A few years ago my oldest was close to graduating from high school. My husband and I always let our children take the Eucharist before us,

so they obviously get back to the pew first. One of my favorite memories is making my way back to the pew and seeing all four of my children kneeling in prayer after receiving Communion. I remember thinking how beautiful it was and how fleeting this time together is. Worshipping with my children is my favorite memory.
—*Emily Stickney*

My favorite memory as a Catholic is relatively recent. A little more than a year and a half ago, I met the mother of one of my six-year-old daughter's friends. We were at a ladies' lunch one day, and she casually remarked in front of this group of women who didn't know each other very well that she reads the Bible every day. Me, being somewhat on the reserved side and having gotten out of the habit of sharing my faith with others since my college years, kept my mouth shut, even though I too had been reading the Bible every day. I don't think I had even shared that I was reading the Bible with the women in my church guild!

I felt so guilty for not saying anything that later that evening I texted this woman and said, "LOL, I read the Bible every day too, but I was too Catholic to share that with everyone!" We started to get together more frequently and had some simple faith sharing conversations. She attended Willow Creek Church and told me I should come to church with her sometime. I said to her, "I think when you talk (she had been talking about fasting and meditating), you sound Catholic."

One day she parked her car near my house to pick up her kids from school and without even thinking about it, I ran out and handed her Scott Hahn's book *Rome Sweet Home*. She started to read the book, and a couple of days later she called me and said that she didn't know what was happening but through our conversations and the information presented in the book, she was feeling called to the Catholic Church.

I became her sponsor, and before we knew it, she had found another friend of ours to join her, and that friend had a friend join the RCIA group, and another woman from my guild who wasn't Catholic (we had no idea!) decided to join as well. To make a long story short, my new favorite memory as a Catholic is bonding with these four women through the RCIA process and standing with them during the Easter Vigil a couple weeks ago, where I witnessed a baptism and their confirmations.

—*Kate Eichstadt*

As I stood behind my goddaughter with my hand on her shoulder as she was confirmed, the bishop lay his hand on her, and I felt a shiver run through me as the Holy Spirit came upon her. Later, she joked that I was shaking, and I replied, "No, Alexa, that was the Holy Spirit!"

—*Ann Herman*

What's your favorite memory as a Catholic?

- Getting to be a flower girl at [my godmother's] wedding. Also, my baptism, even though I don't remember it. (Greta, age nine)
- First Communion and my confirmation! The church was packed, and I got to wear a beautiful dress. (Agnes, age fourteen)
- First Communion, because our whole family was together, even those that don't go to church. (Henry, age twelve)
- Confirmation! It was just awesome. I know that all my

months of service and preparation were being fulfilled that day. (Jonah, age fourteen)

• The "Ave Maria" during our wedding. On a day with so much busy-ness, it was the chance to slow down and just be present in the moment with God and my husband. (Autumn, wife and mom)

• My confirmation so many years ago . . . not only because of the sacrament, but because I could share the day with my grandfather (he died several years ago), who served as my sponsor that day. (Jess, husband and father)

—*The Sweley family*

As a nine-year-old fourth grader in the 1940s, I begged my parents to let me be an altar boy at the Catholic church in our town. My parents reluctantly said yes because we lived in the country, I was the youngest of seven brothers and sisters, and we were quite poor.

I felt very special being an altar boy and being close to the priests and sisters, and I thought God as well, as I served Mass.

In the summer I would serve six o'clock Mass a week or two each month, and my dad would take me to church and stay for Mass. This was his return to becoming a practicing Catholic again, as he had not attended church for many years.

Our family noticed this was changing his life. He stopped using foul language and drinking. My mother and I felt my serving at Mass and his taking me to church each time I served was responsible for his return to Catholicism. My dad was a devout Catholic for the last twenty-two years of his life and a favorite memory of mine growing up Catholic.

—*Name Withheld*

My favorite memory of being a Catholic is probably not what you'd expect as a favorite memory, but it saved my life. I was in a terrible, dark time in my life. I was involved in crime and a total downward spiral of sin. I was arrested and sent to prison. My life in prison did not improve. I committed a crime in prison and was sentenced to twenty-four months in solitary confinement.

In solitary the only books available to read were law books or the Bible. I started slowly reading the Bible, and soon I had read the whole thing and reread it again and again, with more understanding each time. After two years, I was released back into the general prison population. I felt the change in myself, and at the time there was no priest in the prison, so I joined a general Bible study. That wasn't as easy as it sounds. My old prison friends could not accept that I had discovered God, and I was harassed daily. The people I used to eat with threw me off the table and continued to "disown" me. I wasn't allowed to participate in sports or any inmate activity (activities the inmates controlled).

It was a very hard time, but I pushed for a Catholic priest to be brought in, and I continued to pray for this. Finally it happened, and I started a prayer group. In time it grew to thirty people. Mass was held weekly, with one hundred inmates taking part, and the numbers just grew. God saved my life and helped me rediscover my faith in spite of all the jeers and foul language directed toward me. God made me strong to go forward, walk through all of this, and hold my head up. I am proud to be Catholic!!

—*Thomas Earlywine*

My favorite memory as a Catholic is the first time I truly felt the power of confession. I had been going through an insurmountable number of struggles in my life, to the point where I didn't know what to do anymore. Prior to this confession, I never opened up so much to a priest for fear that they would always judge me for my sins. However, I got over this preconception and opened up during confession—and it honestly felt like I was opening up my heart to God. I was also fortunate enough to have had a priest who was able to easily relate my issues to God's teachings. From that moment, it was as if I was given a new pair of eyes. I started looking at my family life differently, my relationships differently, my career differently, nearly everything differently. It's what led me to Dynamic Catholic and to who I am today.

—*Mike Palarz*

My sister and I used to spend several weeks every summer with our great aunt, who was a Dominican sister. Every evening we were allowed to participate in vespers and evening prayers. Even as a ten-year-old, I had the feeling that we were being transported to heaven every night! As the sisters processed in song and holding candles, I was certain I was among the heavenly angels adoring God. When my time here is finished, I hope I will be processing with them to glorify the Blessed Trinity. I have carried this memory throughout my earthly journey, and I hope it will be my last thought as I leave this world.

—*Denis Beck*

I am a cradle Catholic, but understanding my faith has been a huge undertaking. I didn't set out to know, love, and serve God. I started out simply going to Mass to keep my parents happy. Along the way I married and started a family. And then, sadly, my second child died in her sleep one day.

The loss was a brick wall of suffering. I was only twenty-four years old, and my life had crumbled into a massive black hole of confusion and pain that just wouldn't go away. At the funeral Mass of the Angels, the priest prayed that my child's soul would be taken to heaven soon. "What do you mean, SOON?" I thought in a panic. "Where is she NOW?"

This tragedy was the wake-up call for me. I was angry, I was hurting, and I was desperately looking for answers. I felt I would never be happy again. I had begged God for my daughter's life as my husband attempted to resuscitate her. No one could have prayed with more sincerity. I knocked, but Christ did not open that door.

So I was alone. No one could understand. No one could help. Not even my husband could reach me. I lived that way for years . . .

The year 1996 found me overwhelmed. I now had four children, but my life felt empty. My husband's job kept him away for 180 days a year. We had surgically altered my husband to limit our family, and it spoiled our marriage.

One day at Mass, the priest announced that he was bringing perpetual Adoration to our parish. I had never heard of it, but I was looking forward to getting an hour away from home one day a week. I signed up—seriously, it was to get out of the house. But God had other plans.

Alone in the chapel at 3:00 a.m., with my Lord. Peace . . . As the weeks passed, my faith grew. I began reading good books, with solid Catholic teaching. I finally understood the value of prayer. I met many people who knew so much more than I did, and who shared their knowledge with me. One man had formerly been a surgeon who did vasectomies. As reparation for his own sin, he reversed my husband's vasectomy for free! Our Lord surrounded me with people of faith, and quietly awakened in me a desire to know, love, and serve God. I hungered for the Eucharist, but I now understood that I needed to go to confession first. I will never be able to express my gratitude, or my joy. It's never abated ... The Catholic Church grounded me.

By the grace of God, we were given another child, our sixth. We called her Mary Victoria, after Our Lady's victory over sin in our lives. We celebrate our thirty-ninth wedding anniversary this year.

I can face anything in life now. I am never alone. Deo gratias! —*Name Withheld*

Clinging to my godmother's forearms, I carefully stepped into my white dress. She zipped up the dress from behind, and it clicked into its final resting place. I spun in circles as giggles and squeals escaped me. The dress fit as if it were designed just for me; its sequins and jewels sparkled and shimmered so much it might as well have belonged to Cinderella. My godmother proceeded to delicately curl my hair and pin it just right. For the finishing touch, she secured my white lace flower veil upon my head. She took one look at me and beamed, "Could you be any more beautiful?"

Hours later was the moment I had been preparing, praying, and waiting for. It was the moment that would define my faith journey and transform my life forever, whether I totally comprehended the magnitude of the occasion or not. As I approached the altar, my white heels anxiously clicked on the stone floor. I was bursting at the seams with excitement. When it was time,

I stood, hands outstretched, ready to receive Jesus for the first time. With a confident "Amen," I accepted Jesus and his grace.

Navigating my way to the chalice, I pronounced another fearless "Amen" and delicately took a sip. Well, really, it was more of a swig than a sip, and it sent me into an uncontrollable coughing fit. Between raspy breaths and tears, I shouted to my mom in the middle of Communion that I needed water. If looks could send you straight to heaven's gates, then the glare my mom gave me would have. Almost instantly, she whisked me away out the back of the church to the water fountain, trying to avoid any further public embarrassment. By the time I got my cough under control and dried my tears, I could hear the congregation singing the closing hymn.

I was *that kid*. I am still that kid, the one whose life seems to be so crazy, comical, and chaotic. I am still a beautiful, hot mess of a girl. Amidst the craziness, comedy, and chaos, you will find a person who is simply imperfect. You know where else you'll find me and countless other imperfect people? The Catholic Church. Because the Church was not founded for those who are perfect and have it all together. Jesus came for the sinners, the imperfect. Jesus comes every Mass in the Eucharist for you and for me.
—*Alex Breindel*

I grew up in a house where we went to a Baptist church for several years, then my parents decided to become members of a non-denominational church when I was in high school. After heading off to college I didn't feel any sense of obligation to attend a church at all, and neither did any of my friends. While I was trying to figure out who I was and what I wanted to do in life, God and religion never entered the equation. All the while my mom continued going to church, reading the Bible, and praying daily. I would go to church with her occasionally out of a sense of loyalty to her.

After graduating and beginning my career, a miracle happened: I met the most wonderful man on earth. While we were dating, he didn't pressure me to go to Mass, but he went every Sunday and would talk to me about what it was like. Eventually I started attending with him. What struck me most was how welcoming everyone was.

Our love grew, and when he proposed, I thought I was in a dream. How lucky was I to meet a loving, devoted man like this! As time went on, though, I realized there was something missing from my life, even with a wonderful career and husband.

The next fall I entered RCIA, with a ton of encouragement from the teachers and parish community. What a powerful, rewarding experience! The night of the Easter Vigil I was baptized and confirmed and celebrated the Eucharist. Words cannot describe how powerful and emotional an experience that was for me.

I relive that experience on a grand scale every year during the Triduum, but in reality, I relive it every Sunday. Jesus Christ has forever changed me, and I am jealous of everyone new I see coming through RCIA each year. I hope I can be an example for those who are not sure they want to be Catholic and encourage them.
—*Amy Obremski*

During Advent of 2016 I reached an all-time low with my depression. Sleep was difficult. I decided instead of lying in bed awake to get up and read spiritual books my priest recommended. He gave us all a copy of *Resisting Happiness*. I soon realized that I was seeking spiritual growth. One thing Matthew Kelly mentioned was to take in an extra Mass weekly. I researched Mass times in our small city and found the motherhouse for the Sisters of St. Joseph.

The first time I went, the entrance song, "The Summons," caught me and I actually burst into tears. I fumbled my way through that Mass, and one of the sweet nuns behind me helped me. I have always idolized my grandparents' devotion to the Catholic faith, but known I needed to make it my own. I prayed to them at that Mass for help. The recessional was their favorite, "Celtic Alleluia," and I knew then where I needed to be every Wednesday afterward.

That same nun has taught me as my new spiritual director that there is no such thing as coincidence . . . only small miracles. I have now read several of Matthew Kelly's books, and I've organized a book group with six people at my work. Two have come back to Mass.

The Catholic faith is meant to be shared. The more we read about, talk about, and write about Jesus, the more alive he is within our own selves. I now see Jesus everywhere . . . even in the public school where I teach kindergarten. (If Jesus is within each of us, he cannot be kept out of public schools.) Jesus, to me, is unconditional love that is felt whenever and wherever we are. I hope this beautiful gift I received is always how I am viewed by my students and everyone else in my life.

—*Beth Castilleja*

My favorite memory is pretty recent. Over the past year I have found myself in such a wonderful place with my faith. I credit Dynamic Catholic for this. It started while reading *Resisting*

Happiness. In 2017 I had my first "Best Lent Ever" experience. Next, I had my first "Best Advent Ever" and absolutely loved reading the *Beautiful Hope* book. Finally, this past Lent I participated in "Best Lent Ever" and attended my first parish mission. Fr. Larry Richards was the guest, and I have no words to describe the life-changing effects his preaching has had on me! When Lent was over, I had a sadness that it was over, like a vacation ending, or the letdown of Christmas season ending. My husband even commented to me that he had noticed I had an amazing Lent, and that he hasn't ever really seen anyone have so much anticipation and joy for the season.

—*Jillian Faith Dureska*

I am privileged to be a Eucharistic minister who is allowed to offer Communion services at the maximum security prison for men in the neighboring town. The men range in age from teenagers to those in their eighties, some of whom will die in this prison. I used to be amazed at the presence of God in some of these men, but the longer I serve there, the more I am sure that God has a special presence in prison. It seems that every week one of the men reveals the presence of God in their lives, whether it is their reflection on the readings or words of encouragement to each other.

Once, when we were offering prayers of petition, one of the inmates said, "Let us pray for our victims, not that they will forgive us, but that they may find healing and be whole again." He continued with the thought that the prisoners may never be forgiven, but they don't need to be. They are guilty of their crimes. The injured deserve a better life then these men handed to them. The rest of the men all agreed with him and asked God to help the victims.

These murderers and rapists treat me with the greatest respect and appreciation. They are kind and caring to each other and to me. I never dwell on their crimes but only on where they are in their faith journey now and how they can help each other to reach their potential as brothers in Christ.

Without the Eucharist I would feel like a kind person who is visiting them, but bringing them the Eucharist to me is a different kind of joy. It makes a stronger community of love and support, a unity of the forgotten who may have done terrible things but who were able to return to humanity in the love of God.

—*Kathryn Poston*

When I was eleven and my brother Brian was five, my parents gave us permission to have a "sleepover" night in the double bed they'd just given me as part of a new bedroom set. Both of them tucked us in as we giggled excitedly, but my father was the last to leave the room. As he touched our heads and said his usual "Good night, sweet dreams, God bless you, I love you," he added, "Don't forget your prayers—add one for rain tonight. We could really use some." Once he left, Brian and I said our regular prayers, then decided to pray to the Virgin Mary in particular for help with much needed rain. We'd only just finished when we began to hear hard drops on the rooftop. They were sporadic at first; then the downpour began. Brian and I stared through the dark at each other with amazed eyes; then, joyfully smiling, we snuggled together and fell asleep. Since that moment, Mary's quiet love of not only Jesus, but all her children, has always been abundantly clear to me. Of course, as an adult, my prayers have expanded far beyond asking for help with rain, but I always feel peace in knowing she listens closely and intercedes on my behalf often.

—*Lisa Fernandi Braddam*

When I was first married, in 1974, I taught at the local Catholic elementary school. I taught there for five years and then moved on to the public schools nearby, where I taught for a total of thirty-six years. When I compare the two experiences, I have to say that the Catholic school years were the most rewarding. The children were dedicated to their studies and their faith. They accepted one another and encouraged each other positively. The parent support was also amazing. I knew they were always with me and helped whenever they were needed. Near my last day for the summer in 1976, my adorable first-grade students and parents surprised me with a baby shower for my first child. The students kept the secret and were so pleased with their surprise. Recently I saw some of the students, and they even remembered that time and asked about my son, who is now forty-two.

After retiring, I attended Mass on Sunday morning and noticed a part-time technology teaching position at the local Catholic middle school. My husband had cancer, but it was under control, and I felt a new calling. After praying to God about this possible new endeavor, I attentively listened and responded when God encouraged me to apply for the position. I submitted my application and waited. I was offered the teaching position, and once again, the students, parents, and staff were supportive and welcomed me to the "family" with open arms and hearts. As my husband's cancer became more serious, the staff and students surrounded me with comfort and held me and my husband in their prayers. The students even led an all-school rosary—what an amazing act of faith!

I know that God had a plan for me to enter the Catholic school arena again. I had come full circle in my teaching career, and I was home. I am ever grateful that I listened to God's direction for me and my life. I am stronger in my faith because of the direction I took. I can truthfully say that God is great and knows what is best for me. Glory to God!

—*Susan Wood*

My favorite memory as a Catholic (aside from the great memories I have from when I was an altar boy) happened last year. I went to a Marriage Encounter Weekend and fell in love with my wife of almost thirty-four years now—and with God—all over again. I learned the true meaning of the sacrament of matrimony, and my wife, Anna, God, and I all became one as it was intended back in 1984. How humbling, beautiful, and alarming it all was! Learning together about life, communication, and even death really woke us up. Every aspect of the weekend was so spiritual, and the love in the room was unbelievable.

—*Hector Zayas*

I went to Catholic school when I was growing up in the Philadelphia suburbs. I have warm memories of a strong bond among the parishioners, priests, Immaculate Heart of Mary Sisters, and lay teachers, and I often regret not sending my own children to Catholic school. When I look back, one sister stands out to me; I'm not sure if it was because it was not a particularly good academic year for me or because she reached out to me, genuinely and patiently wanting me to understand the subject matter. Years later what I remember is her disposition—her internal happiness, the glow about her that was contagious. Even as a child, I thought, *I want to be that happy. But what makes her so happy? What is she doing that keeps her so positive and energetic and caring?*

It wasn't until many years later when I thought of this sister and realized that the Lord was showing himself to me little by little and teaching me what a life devoted to him was like. Sometimes during the hectic days of family and work commitments, I think, *What would life be like if I served the Lord her way?* I quickly realize that everyone has a purpose, and mine is to be the-best-version-of-myself as a wife, mother, sister, daughter . . . and disciple.

—Lizanne Kile

A favorite memory is being at Los Angeles Religious Ed. Congress and meeting Matthew Kelly for a brief moment, shaking his hand to thank him for the "fifteen minutes in the classroom of God" talk that had motivated me to grow up in Catholicism. Feeling his tiredness, I prayed for him that day, and I have remained in prayer for his endeavors, which led to my interest in the Dynamic Catholic Institute and the Ambassador Program.

—Lorraine Villegas

My most poignant and treasured memory as a Catholic was during the spring semester of 2007, while studying abroad through Franciscan University in Austria. I was given the opportunity to serve in Lourdes in the baths during Holy Week, and experience the peace and healing of our Blessed Mother. What an honor it was to see the faith of the women who came to the baths, praying and hoping for spiritual and physical healing for all the suffering they carried in their hearts and bodies.

Every day I would walk past the grotto with candles burning brightly with prayer intentions from all over the world, and felt that universal sense of family and belonging. In many ways Lourdes felt like a coming home, and it was the first time I felt the love our Blessed Mother had for me, and for all of the world. She called me there for some purpose, and that purpose was to learn to love her.

As the years have gone by, the fruit of that initial encounter with her has grown and blossomed into a deep abiding relationship that I treasure more with each passing day. She is my friend, my comfort, my prayer warrior, my intercessor, my peace, and my teacher. Ultimately though, Mary is my mother, and I know that there is nothing I could say or do that could make her love me less.
—*Elizabeth Kuhn*

The day I first felt the Holy Spirit fill my heart and bring me a serenity I had never known is the most memorable day as a Catholic for me. After years of living my life worrying about pleasing others, I now look forward to a future where I will live for pleasing Jesus and surrendering myself to his will. My heart is just filled with joy to know he really loves me and I will always have his grace in my life.
—*Allan Gaherty*

My favorite memory is time spent with a family friend, Sister Regina, a nun with the order of the Poor Clares. She took an immediate liking to me. She entered the convent in her early twenties, and was "Mother Superior" of her order three times.

One of the last times I saw her alive was on a visit to Omaha, where her convent was located. She was in her early nineties at the time. She hugged me . . . and said she would keep me in prayer . . . and handed me her rosary, which she'd had all those years in the convent, and told me she wanted me to have it. My goodness, can you imagine all the prayers said on that rosary over all those many, many years? There is great deal of spiritual power in that rosary, which I still have and use to this very day. Whenever I begin the rosary on those beads, I look up and say with a smile on my face, "Sr. Regina, come on, let's pray together."
—*Jim Mumaugh*

My favorite memory is the first time I realized that Jesus had "spoken" to me. I was sitting quietly in the back of a church, lamenting all of my problems, when my eyes were "directed" to the crucifix, and I experienced Jesus answering my questions. A flush came over my whole body. I'll never forget it.

Another profound memory was actually experiencing a "miracle" when the car I was driving during a blinding rain began to swerve. Right before it was going to smash into a highway divider, the car stopped on a dime on the left shoulder, out of traffic. The first sound I heard after the car stopped was that of the rosary, which had been in my lap, flying across the front of the car and landing on the passenger side floor. I stared at that rosary on the floor, realizing that the Blessed Mother, my guardian angel, and a whole host of heavenly protectors had taken care of me and wanted me to know there was no other explanation for the car stopping the way it did.
—*Denise Frederick*

My favorite memory was attending my first Christ Renews His Parish (Welcome) weekend. It changed me from a one-hour-a-week Catholic to a full-time Catholic, with all the wonderful benefits that come with having our Lord and Savior as my best friend.

—Vince Turnquist

One of my favorite Catholic memories was the result of a one-day Catholic Men's Fellowship (CMF) conference in 2000. In the decade preceding the year 2000, I was an uninvolved Catholic, going to Mass but doing little else. Toward the end of the decade I began to feel restless, feeling I should be doing more.

In 2000 I heard of a CMF conference with two nationally known speakers: Fr. Benedict Groeschel and Chuck Colson. Days before the conference I tried to get a ticket but was told to get my ticket at the door.

Little did I know God's plan for me. Without a ticket, I drove to Cincinnati the day before the conference. At the motel, my bill was reduced by a third due to a motel promotion. In the morning of the conference, I found a parking spot cheaper than I expected. While walking to the conference, the thought came to me: "Don't take the first offer, take the second one." A man approached me saying "Here's a ticket for twenty-five dollars." Another man said: "Why take that one when you could have this one for free!" I took the second ticket.

The first speaker of the conference was unknown to me, a young Matthew Kelly. He told many engaging stories, but one stood out to me. It was the story of Fred, a man bored with the Mass. One Sunday God spoke to him: "If you want to be happy, this coming week do this and stop doing that." But Fred did not take God's advice. Week after week God said the same thing to Fred. Finally God said to Fred: "You won't get lesson two until you complete lesson one!"

Fr. Benedict Groeschel and Chuck Colson gave excellent talks in the afternoon. So I bought the tape set of conference talks. During my four-hour drive home to North Canton, Ohio, I listened to the three talks. But my fondest memory of my trip occurred when I realized God's plan was to hear Matthew Kelly's talk. His message was that God wants the best for me and God's call is a call to joy. The story of Fred touched me. It was time for me to get to lesson two.

As a result of my trip, I had a meeting with the pastor of the church I attended. In that meeting I described the story of Fred, I made a confession, and asked to become a parishioner. The pastor agreed and gave me some good advice. Then he asked me to help schedule lay ministers for the weekend Mass. As scheduler, I met more than ninety parishioners who became my friends. I became part of the parish community.

There were other changes. I became a member of the liturgy committee and the adult faith formation committee. I gained an appreciation of the teaching of the Church by reading and studying the Holy Bible and the *Catechism of the Catholic Church*. I gained an appreciation of the Mass by participating as scheduler, lector, and altar server. And I began telling those I met: "Have a joyful day," since God's call is a call to joy.
—*Frederick G. Carty*

My favorite memory is visiting a young Jewish man with cancer who was a hospice patient. I was his hospice volunteer. After a number of visits with him, he told me he would like to become a Catholic. I felt a little shaky in helping him move toward that goal, because his parents berated me for even suggesting such a thing to their dying son.

As lovingly as I could, I assured them that this was totally his decision. Calls from their rabbi outlining how I was hurting this already-hurting family came more than once. I kept assuring everyone that I was not suggesting his conversion but was only witnessing to my own faith.

He converted to Catholicism three weeks before he died and was convinced he had made the right decision. When he asked me to take part in his funeral service *and* deliver the eulogy, I didn't know what to expect from his family. But when the rite of Christian burial was over, both his parents embraced and thanked me. I will always remember this.

—*John DiMaggio*

While my father was dying, I was working on knitting him a shawl (he was always cold due to his illness, but I thought I was going to make him warm; funny what we think we can change!). I didn't get it finished in time, so after my father died I just put it away. After a while I realized I could present it to my younger sister, who had taken such wonderful care of Dad. She was so touched that I thought I would start a prayer shawl ministry in my small parish.

My pastor was extremely receptive, but after a few announcements in the bulletin, no one responded. I was getting discouraged, but Fr. Kris said, "Set the date for your first meeting and they will come." I am happy to say that was eight years ago now, and the same eight faith-filled ladies who showed up that first

night are as committed as ever to our ministry. When my pastor said, "They will come," I think of Jesus, who said, "Follow me."
—*Marilyn Schwasta*

My favorite memory as a Catholic is one of forgiveness. My first reconciliation was when I was a father of four and in my thirties. I remember writing down my sins on a paper (for thirty-plus years) so I wouldn't forget something big. I remember my jaw shaking as I read the sins to the priest and how humbling it was. What I remember most, though, is when the priest did the absolution—how the weight from all the sins was lifted off my shoulders, and I really felt forgiveness in a mental and physical way. I walked out hardly feeling my own body weight and extremely thankful and in awe.
—*Greg Kaiser*

My baptism is my favorite memory. I came to the Lord late in life, and through my baptism I have been given new life. I remember at one of Matthew Kelly's events he talked about being transformed and what it means to each of us. He talked about how some of us want to be tweaked and not really transformed. This strengthened my resolve for change and transformation, and showed me that I have choices, and the choice I want is to be what God wants me to be. My baptism has led to many new things in my life that I am so grateful for!
—*Kathy Greene*

All my memories come under the title of "family." I love remembering how, when my grandma would come to visit, my mother

and father, my six sisters, and my brother would sit in the living room saying the rosary in the afternoon. I love that my whole family went to church together every Sunday and took up a whole pew. And I love that I have been able to share my faith with my boys, who seem to "get it" too!
—*Name Withheld*

My favorite memory was on a Holy Thursday several years ago. When the sanctuary light was extinguished, for some reason I felt such a profound sadness. I had watched this happen at Mass on Holy Thursday for years, but on that night I actually felt how sad and lonely Jesus must have felt on that night two thousand years ago. It might seem strange that this would be a favorite memory, but I never want to lose the absolute closeness I felt to Jesus that night.
—*Gerri Stanko*

Favorite memory: Pope Francis' visit to Philadelphia. I volunteered to assist handicapped people. I was assigned to a non-Catholic woman with cancer . . . and she was cured!
—*Toni Saldutti*

I have been a cradle Catholic all my life. When I was growing up, going to church and being Catholic mostly seemed to be an obligation. It was sandwiched between having to do chores at home and working in the family business. My mother was a schoolteacher, and my father owned a liquor store in the poorest neighborhood of Detroit. My three brothers and I took turns working there, but it was too dangerous for my sisters. At twelve years old

I was finally big enough to fit into the bulletproof vest we took turns wearing (we only had one to share between the four of us).

While I was in medical school, I helped care for my father, who was a patient at the hospital where I was training to become a doctor. After he finally succumbed to the ravages of vascular disease, diabetes, and heart failure, I took a sabbatical and studied a master's degree in English literature at University of Edinburgh in Scotland. I traveled the world seeking enlightenment in experiences, studies, art, philosophy, music, and worldly pursuits. I also did a great many things ostensibly for the greater good—I cared for thousands of patients and did international relief work for years in inner cities. I did what seemed to be many good things by all accounts from the outside looking in. But I did not do them with Christ as my center.

That only came after a very profound experience during a critical time in my life, during the sacrament of reconciliation, when I clearly realized it was a sacrament and not simply a psychological catharsis.

Only now, just after the midpoint of my life, do I realize that being Catholic is the blueprint for being happy. I used to pray to have the conviction of a born-again Christian. Now I am utterly convicted of the truth, power, and beauty of the Catholic Church. And I want to bring people to it through my actions.

—*Dr. Gary Sarafa*

It's hard to pick just one memory, but I would say a 1995 men's weekend retreat called Christ Renews His Parish (Welcome). It was a very moving and life-changing experience and got me started on praying the rosary daily.

—*Mike Munn*

My favorite memory of being Catholic is attending Catholic schools and witnessing the example of the good Dominican nuns who sacrificed and gave so generously of themselves and lived such simple lives.

—*Helen Lehner*

A favorite memory is attending Good Friday services with my beloved grandmother. My dear grandmother, who lived to be ninety, is one of my inspirations for being a devout Catholic. After my grandfather died, I always made sure I was not working on Good Friday. I would buy my grandmother some Easter flowers, drive to her house, and then bring her to church. Together, we would venerate the cross. These experiences brought us closer together. After the service, we would visit my grandfather's grave and then return to her house for her homemade Manhattan Clam Chowder. I will cherish these memories forever.

Another favorite memory is performing a "Living Rosary" in sixth grade. Even all these years later, I still remember the peace and excitement I felt as the ceremony approached my "bead." As a young boy whose voice was late in changing, I was often ashamed to speak aloud in front of a group. But on that day, I spoke my Hail Mary loud and clear! This is the inspiration of our Catholic faith!

—*James Wren*

Being only seventeen years old and a junior in high school has a lot of ups and downs. But I have two memories I will remember for the rest of my life as a Catholic daughter of Christ.

I have been going to Steubenville St. Paul for almost four years now. It's a three-day summer camp in Minnesota where Catholics from all across the country come together to praise Jesus. One year, I went up to one of my friends who I could tell was *not* okay. I pulled him aside and we just talked. Now, this friend of mine is a quiet kid; he doesn't talk much and he doesn't like talking about God to anyone. But once we were alone, he started crying and talking about how much he loved this place and didn't want to leave. He knew that once we were home, he was going to go back to his old self. I told him he didn't have to go back to his old self—he could come with me to Mass or Adoration anytime. Ever since that day, I've fallen in love with being a Catholic, and I don't care who knows, or who judges me for it.

The second memory is the time a priest visited our youth group and talked to us about being Catholic and spreading our faith to everybody around us. I go to a public school and there aren't many Catholics or Christians at our school. But there is a Catholic school right across the river from our school, and this priest said that that was the school we should be going to. One of my friends spoke up and said, "If we go to this Catholic school, who's going to be the one that spreads the Catholic faith in our school?" I realized he was right, and this also helped me to live my Catholic faith even when people might judge me.

These two experiences have helped me become the person I am today.

—*McKayla Marie Swallow*

When I was a little girl, a nun told me, "Whenever you feel afraid, just reach out your hand and ask Jesus to hold it." I have done that since I was six years old, and I have always told my children and grandchildren to do the same thing. I close my eyes, and I see him

right there with me, holding my hand. I get a peace and comfort that cannot be denied. My daughters and grandkids say the same thing.
—*Gerry Short*

My favorite memory is my marriage to my wife, Suzanne. God truly helped me to choose the person to help make me complete and bring me closer to him. We have been married fifty-three years and yet it seems like our wedding was only yesterday. As all couples we have our ups and downs, but we never go to sleep without holding hands and praying to God. I know he's listening!
—*Marv Marek*

My favorite memory is a recent one. I'm a cradle Catholic, and my wife is a convert. Five years ago my wife came home from RCIA (as a sponsor) and slammed a copy of the *Catechism* down in front of me and said, "You need to read this. You're supposed to be the spiritual leader of this family." That week I read it cover to cover and was immediately renewed in my faith, all due to the man teaching RCIA, my wife, and that book. I'm currently finishing my first of five years of training to be a deacon.
—*Bob Denne*

My favorite memory as a Catholic is praying the Novena (de Aguinaldos) every day from December 16 to Christmas Eve. My family is Colombian, and this is a beautiful tradition practiced by Colombian Catholics. The children gather with musical instruments, and after the prayers for the day, everyone sings songs (*villancicos*) in hopeful anticipation of Christmas! As a child, I loved doing this because it gave me the opportunity to see my cousins daily. Today, I look fondly on these memories and reflect on the beauty of knowing that in one country in this huge world, there are faithful Catholics who are singing the same exact songs and praying the same words, to give glory to our heavenly king!

—*Nora Gonzalez*

Eighteen years ago my husband died of a heart attack while he was driving with me in the car. I did not go to church after that for almost ten years. I went to work to France, and one of my friends asked me to meet her in Paris and take her to Lourdes. I said, "Okay, my friend, I will take you, but please don't make me go to church."

As soon we arrived, we took our bags to the hotel and walked around the town. It was around 8:30 p.m., but she insisted that we go to the grotto because Mass was being celebrated at 12:00 a.m. in Spanish. I told her she was crazy, that I was tired and wanted to go to sleep. She insisted that God would give me the strength to come and see the grotto.

We arrived just in time for Mass to start at the grotto. It started raining hard right then too. As I was standing in front of the grotto, looking up at the sky with the rain coming down, I had a sensation I had never felt before in my life. I started to cry and asked for forgiveness from God, Christ, and his mother. Since that moment, my life has been changed completely. Being Catholic is like a burning sensation that can't be explained, where you feel God inside you.

—*Isolda Iznaga*

My favorite memory as a Catholic was going to confession for the first time in forty-eight years, and feeling (and actually seeing) Jesus there welcoming me home. This changed my life forever, and has made my path to heaven look so clear. I must add that I believe reading the book *Rediscovering Catholicism* is why I found myself in that confessional after all those years and all those sins. I thank you now and will thank you in heaven.

—*Kevin Quinn*

My favorite memory growing up Catholic from my childhood is the incredibly close connection we had with our parish priests. They were like family and attended all our holiday events.

—*Michelle Merlini*

Every day is a new and favorite memory when you're truly doing God's will.

—*Gwen Valentine*

My favorite memory as a Catholic is being in the Holy Land and walking to and seeing the places where Jesus walked and lived. Entering the tomb and the upper room was life changing. I still tear up just thinking about that trip. I wish every Catholic could make that trip and really feel the holiness and humanness of our Lord and his mother.

—*Mary Starz*

My favorite memory as a Catholic is the story of my relationship with Monsignor Daniel B. Logan. He was the president of my high school. As a student and a teenager who knew it all, I judged him and how he ran the school very harshly. In my senior year, I was on the newspaper staff, and I wrote a scathing article about him. After high school, I didn't encounter him again until five years later when I had gotten married and moved into his parish.

I was terrified to go to Mass. I told my husband there was no way I could go to church at his parish. I gave it a try and was amazed that Monsignor welcomed me with open arms. He was thrilled we were part of his parish, and I went on to participate in many ministries—Eucharistic Minister, RCIA sponsor, parish council member. I asked Monsignor one day if he remembered the article I had written in high school. His response was that he did not remember and didn't want to remember. The only memory he had of me in high school was that I was a liturgical assistant who came most mornings before school and set up for Mass in the school chapel.

I was awestruck that this man chose to forgive, chose not remember the bad, and chose only to remember the good. He truly lived the example of Jesus. He had forgiven long before I sought to ask for it. To this day we are good friends, and he has shown me that there are warriors for Christ among us.

—*Delia Kavanaugh*

I attended the World Meeting of Families in Philadelphia with Pope Francis in 2015. Outside of the the Cathedral Basilica of Saints Peter and Paul was a prayer station. Here, each person was to get a piece of cloth and write on it their prayer request. They then tied it to the fence, and removed another person's cloth to pray for, before hanging it back in a different area. It was incredible to see so many pieces of cloth, so many prayer requests hanging outside the basilica! I still remember the moment I read the request I got to pray for: "Lord, help me see light through the darkness of debt." So simple, yet so powerful; I was in tears praying for this person I had never met.

When Pope Francis traveled around to greet the crowds, he made a special stop there to walk into the area with the prayer requests, and offer his intentions as the Holy Father for all the prayer requests. There were probably close to a million. Very powerful!

—*Alton Lee*

My fondest memory of being Catholic is how, after being away from the Church for several years, a priest who heard my confession welcomed me back warmly! He didn't berate or lecture me. His words meant more than he will ever know. I knew it was Jesus himself welcoming me back.

—*Kathy Sechler*

My favorite memory of being Catholic is in my youth going to Mass with my grandparents and parents—feeling the excitement of possibly being chosen to bring up the gifts or just knowing that after a Saturday evening Mass we would all have dinner together. I loved the way it was unspoken that you knew your family would be together.

—*Cyndi Shah*

I was in Florida in a very poor section of the state, looking for a local church to attend Sunday Mass. I asked my father-in-law and his girlfriend to come with me. You could tell by the parishioners how truly poor the area was. It was one of the most moving Masses we have ever attended. My father-in-law's girlfriend started crying; my father-in-law took the priest aside after Mass to tell him how beautiful the Mass was, and I wrote the priest the same thing upon returning home. I cannot pinpoint what it was, but we truly felt the Holy Spirit working through these people. It was beautiful!

—*Name Withheld*

One day after Mass, I became upset talking to my church friends about my husband Dave's recent diagnosis of stage four cancer. It is still hard for me to talk about without crying, but it was especially difficult early on when the shock was so raw and new. I was alone in the car because Dave had decided to let his body get some well deserved rest and stayed home that day.

As I was driving home, I became more and more upset, and soon I was sobbing. I was crying so hard that I really should not have been driving; I could barely see where I was going. Suddenly my thoughts turned from despair and darkness toward Jesus. I said out loud, "Jesus, I trust in you." I said it again. Then I noticed I was no longer sobbing. I repeated the phase "Jesus, I trust in you" over and over again. By the time I got two miles down the road, I was calm and under control. Thank you, Lord! Truly amazing! "Jesus, I trust in you" has become my mantra of recent days. I have learned to repeat that phase, to have it in my heart always.

—*Linda Darby*

When I went through Christ Renews His Parish (Welcome) in 2009, I had stopped practicing as a Catholic for a number of years. I felt comforted, accepted without judgment, and loved by the members of my CRHP group. It felt like coming home, and it still does.

—*Rick Bartel*

My favorite memory is when I was about four years old and my mom and dad brought me into the church where I grew up and, in front of the tabernacle, my dad showed me how to genuflect. My mom leaned down and whispered in my ear: "Shaun, that's God's house . . . Jesus is inside there." This great sense of awe and wonder came over me—I'll never forget that!
—*Fr. Shaun Foggo*

My favorite memory as a Catholic is a recent one. I walked the Camino with a Dynamic Catholic–led pilgrimage. It was the most spiritual journey of my life. I am not typically a very social person. I expected the Camino to be a journey to be alone with God. Although I got that in an incredibly special way, I got so much more. Besides the real experience of walking with what seemed to be a material Jesus, I found him in the people I walked with. For me, the whole experience was as close as I can imagine to heaven on earth. Celebrating Mass, searching for Christ, together with fellow pilgrims, talking about our faith, living our faith, and sharing in our pain in a very real way was a beautiful thing.
—*Doug Monckton*

My youngest daughter Allison, who is now eighteen and leaving for college in the fall, is and always has been the most spiritual person I have ever encountered, even in utero. She was always very calm, a little kick here and there or a little bump now and then just to let us know she was doing well. On Sundays it was more of the same, until I set foot in our church for Sunday Mass. This child would immediately start doing back flips! My tummy would be visibly moving; it was constant and deliberate. It gave both my husband and me great joy. She loved being at church then, and she continues to love and attend to this day.

In late February 2007 my forty-nine-year-old sister Sherry was diagnosed with stage four lung cancer and given three months to live. On June 1, 2007, I drove to St. Agnes Parish School to pick Allison up from second grade; we had to fly from California to Michigan. It had been three months, and true to their word, my sister was gone. Allison could see that I had been crying and wanted to know why I was so sad. When we arrived home I tried the best I could to explain to my second grader that I was sad for the loss of my sister, and I was sad for her husband and their children. I told her I would really miss being able to see my sister, and that was why I was so upset. This child of eight years old took her mother by the hand, looked straight into her eyes, and said, "Don't be sad, Momma! Today is Aunt Sherry's LUCKY day—now she gets to live with Jesus!" She was so excited—in her mind there was nothing to be sad about; this is to be celebrated! Aunt Sherry was now living with Jesus, and it doesn't get any better than that! My very young and very wise daughter was the one that provided comfort during this time as she reminded me of Jesus' promise.

When a dear friend of mine passed away, also at the age of forty-nine, leaving a husband and young children, her mother was devastated. I shared Allison's words of wisdom with her. Weeks later Allison and I received the most heartfelt thank-you note ever. This mother now celebrates her daughter's LUCKY day every year.

—*Connie Munden*

The event that really turned me on to our faith and got me fired up was Cursillo about twenty years ago. It was a watershed in my life. I have been involved in a weekly group since then, and it really reinforces my faith.

—*Jim Cannon*

I was a cradle Catholic, but hadn't practiced for nearly twenty years. Then, after ten years of marriage, and definitely not by my urging, my wife decided to become Catholic. She began bringing home questions and comments from her RCIA meetings, which drew me back into the faith. The Holy Spirit at work! That was thirty years ago.

—*Robert Hapner*

I was six years old, and our family had just become Catholic. After spending kindergarten in a public school, I transferred to St. Mary's for first grade. One Sunday morning I was playing with my model cars under the elm tree by the road when my mother can out on the front porch and said, "Dickie, it's time to come in and get ready for Mass." I said, "I'm not going today, Mother." She said, "You're not! How come?" I repeated something I learned from Sister in class the previous week. "I don't have to go to Mass because I haven't reached the 'age of reason' yet." My wise mother replied, "You just did!" I went in, got ready, and have been going to Mass for seventy-five years now. Sometimes you just know too much.

—*Richard "Dickie" Shaw*

My favorite memory was witnessing my dad in the presence of the Eucharist. His simple humble approach throughout Mass showed me he was a grateful servant. During Communion, he was always moved to a place of tearful joy. For him, it was sadness (crucifixion), yet it was joy (resurrection)! Wow. I was amazed.

When I was a child, my dad would spend quiet time meditating with our Lord, unbeknownst to me. I would often interrupt him for some reason or another. But he lovingly took time to talk. And that talk often led to speaking about God. He always said, "Talk to God as your father. He will always listen. Every day spend time with him." And now as an adult, I see why my dad was always at peace.

—*Francine Gabreluk*

I loved being in youth group as a high school student and going on retreats. In a time where my life felt so fake and unsure, the youth group kept me grounded and stopped me from giving in to my selfish desires. It was where I felt known and where I came to know myself. After high school it took me a while to find my place as a part of the Church outside of youth group, as I couldn't reproduce the bond and sense of belonging I felt there. Thankfully after searching and finding Catholic websites, blogs, podcasts, and specifically Dynamic Catholic, I have placed myself in new "groups" that have challenged me to grow in my faith.

—*Kelly Kozlowski*

Thirty-three years ago, when I was fresh out of treatment for alcoholism, I went on a Jesuit Ignatian retreat. For the first time in over ten years, I went to confession. I felt a liberation that is difficult to describe. I cried and smiled at the same time.

—*Mark Rudloff*

My fondest memory of being a Catholic is when my father asked his four sons to attend a weekend silent Jesuit retreat to celebrate his sixtieth birthday. My father recently passed away at eighty-nine. I am fortunate to have attended the retreat with him annually for the majority of those years. The sharing of his faith and the way he lived it were the best blessings a father could have passed on to his son, and I am forever grateful for that gift!
—*Dave Johnston*

When our first grandson was born, my mother was suffering with lung cancer. We very much wanted to her to be present for his baptism, but a few days before the baptism was to take place, my mother took a turn for the worse, and she passed away at home. The next morning after Mass we met with the priest and asked if it would be possible to have the memorial Mass for my mother and the baptism for our grandson on the same day. He said of course, and a few days later we celebrated the full circle of life—first our grandson's baptism, and then the memorial Mass for my mother. To me this was the perfect expression of our Catholic faith, and the love and understanding of a parish priest. We welcomed our grandson into the Catholic family, and followed that with a celebration of my mom's transition to eternal life. It was an emotional day, but in a good way. Everyone who attended said it was truly special.
—*Jim Kipers*

My favorite memory as a Catholic was attending the Triduum at the Franciscan Renewal Center in Scottsdale, Arizona, with my daughter, Jill, who was battling a rare disease. The rendition of

Jesus' passion, death, and resurrection was presented by the community, and the experience was faith-affirming for both of us. It enabled us to move forward in hope, with her eventual passing a year later.

—*Janet Creedon*

My early teenage years were full of questions and doubts about my Catholic faith. But I was especially close to my grandmother, a strong Catholic woman who spoiled me and made the best French toast in the world, and I was heartbroken when she started losing her sight and showing signs of dementia. One Sunday at Mass, I looked over to see a tear running down her cheek during the hymn "Were You There?" Even though she could no longer see and her body was failing, her sorrow at Jesus' passion was as strong as ever. At that moment, I prayed to have her faith my whole life, that I would never become immune to the suffering and pain of Christ, or the suffering and pain of those around me. She is gone now, but my faith and love of Jesus are strong in large part because of her.

—*Sara Gudorf*

Our family attended a Day of Mercy at our church, and we all individually went to confession. After confession our family was gathered in the common area, and my daughter turned to me with excitement in her voice and said, "Mom, I feel like I just talked to Jesus." How cool is that?

—*Kelly Flaherty*

My favorite memory was the comfort I felt as an unwed mother when I attended a local church frequently and prayed to Mary

to help me through that time because of my embarrassment and shame.
—*Name Withheld*

Consecrating myself to the Immaculate Heart of Mary was game changing.
—*Sue Grabowski*

My favorite memory being a Catholic was when I went to Ignited by Truth in Raleigh for the first time. North Carolina isn't predominantly Catholic, although the numbers have grown. I've been to a lot of women's conferences with Beth Moore, but at IBT I was hearing from Bible scholars and Catholic speakers who shared my faith for the first time! I didn't realize that there were people who were celebrating being Catholic and writing about it! I went home with a library of books that have helped me grow in my faith. The opportunity to celebrate confession and Mass and hear all those speakers in one afternoon was so affirming to my faith.
—*Mary Beth Lassiter*

One of my favorite memories of being Catholic is the feeling of "home." I was raised in a family with lots of children, and my parents didn't have a lot of extra money, so for part of our tithe we always gave time and talents to the parish. Specifically, I remember a two-year stint when my parents volunteered our family to be the janitors of the church. We would go to the church every week as a family and clean everything. The most special part of that for me was that even though there were parts of the church that were sacred (and we treated them reverently), there was nothing that was "off limits" or that we had to keep our distance from. It instilled in me a sense of belonging, that this is "my church" and I am part of it. From taking part in the Mass to keeping the building clean and in working order, I was an important part of the Catholic community no matter what age I was, and I always knew, wherever I went, that the Church would be there for me and I had a place to belong.

—*Kimberly Harper*

Years ago, many saw me as a popular university student. Rather than being happy, though, I was miserable and depressed. Death seemed attractive. No matter how much I accomplished, nothing seemed to fill my empty void, or erase my self-hate. Friends, sorority sisters, family, even the school psychologist all tried their best, but to no avail.

Finally, I decided only God could help. I longed for a strong, healing faith. With girlfriends and relatives, I had visited churches of various denominations. Praying for an answer, I suddenly remembered my aunt with whom, years ago, I had attended Mass. She was the first Catholic to join our extended family, and I marveled at her faith. Born with a crippled hip, she never complained. After she married my uncle, she suffered numerous miscarriages before my cousin was born. Still, her faith never wavered. Remembering her now, I recalled how I used to look forward to visiting and attending Mass with her. As we knelt in prayer at Lake Geneva's St. Francis de Sales Catholic Church, peace I hadn't known surrounded me.

I began to study my Catholic friends, including my roommate, and realized how much I admired them. They had something I did not. Their faith had made better people of them. I noticed how caring they were. As I struggled, I especially appreciated their attentive support.

When I started dating my future husband, Bob, we had long discussions about religion and faith. One sunny fall afternoon, as we sat alone in my sorority's living room, Bob said, "I hope you don't mind? Last night, I kept thinking about you, so I wrote this little poem." With a warm smile, he continued, "Remember, I'm studying engineering, not English like you."

Looking at his note, I read the refrain, "Carol is like a leaf floating down a stream."

I sat still, stunned.

"You're not mad or anything?"

"Oh Bob, you understand. I've been trying to please everyone, parents, teachers, and friends. I feel overwhelmed, guilty, and frustrated. It's too much. I don't know which way to go."

"I do understand," Bob said as he wrapped his arms around me.

During the next few weeks, I prayed and thought about our talk. When I listened to the voice inside, I heard, "The Catholic Church will help you find what is important, what God wants." For the first time, I felt embraced by safe boundaries and forgiveness. The Catholic Church was a theology on which I could depend to pardon my guilt. Harming oneself was a sin; I could close the door on those thoughts. I began to feel more alive, almost as if I had once been numbed by frostbite and now was tingling with the warmth of a new faith. I could feel a presence, a love touching me, not for what I did, but who I was. I began taking lessons, and a year later, in front of family and friends, I joined the Catholic

Church. For the first time, I felt safe, secure, and trusting in my new faith.

It has been more than fifty years since I became Catholic. With counseling, prayer, study, and a supportive family, I have a found a miraculous life. It hasn't always been easy being Catholic, nor has it been easy being me. I have made mistakes and had my doubts, but the Catholic Church has always been there to welcome me home.

Now, as I celebrate Mass with Bob, my patient husband of fifty-five years, I pray for our three beautiful daughters, their husbands, and our seven grandchildren. During the summer months, Bob and I help at our rustic, mountain Catholic mission church. We clean, publicize services, lector, distribute Communion, and whatever else is needed at Our Lady of the Lakes, so others may experience the healing faith, hope, and sense of direction I found as a Catholic.

—*Carol Strazer* (*First published in 2008 in* Chicken Soup for the Soul: Living Catholic Faith. *Used with permission.*)

I received my first Communion on May 2, 1959, at St. Bonaventure's Church in Chicago, Illinois. I was a seven-year-old second-grader, one of about sixty kids to receive that day, but, two of us have remained lifelong friends. To this day, Ann and I call each other every May 2 to remember and celebrate this beautiful gift given to us.

—*Sharon Klein*

My dad has lived out the Gospel as a devout and good Catholic man for others all his life. My favorite memory of being with him

was also as a young girl. He was and is a dove—an early-to-bed and early-to-rise man—and so am I. When I was six years old, I remember walking hand-in-hand with him through the park across the street from our home. I felt so loved and protected and full of joy to be in that moment with my dad walking to Saturday morning Mass. I'm one of the lucky people on earth whose earthly father strived every day to be like his heavenly Father.
—*Melissa McGlinn*

My favorite memory is the epiphany I had three years ago that I must turn my life over to God. The doors started opening, and the miracles just keep coming. And when there is fear or suffering, it is not as debilitating and crippling. My chronic depression is virtually gone, and my life is so much easier!
—*Victoria Le Forestier*

My favorite memory is being able to see my daughter who has Down Syndrome receive her first Communion and confirmation at the age of thirty-one after years of thinking she would not be able to because of her disability. Many good people were involved in making this possible. Seeing my daughter receive the living Body and Blood of Christ brings me much joy, knowing she comes into communion with Jesus.
—*Name Withheld*

I live in the metro area of New York, and my favorite memory of being a Catholic was attending Mass the afternoon immediately following the tragedy of 9/11. I was overwhelmed with the realization that the Scriptures, written thousands of years prior to this tragedy, spoke so beautifully of comfort and peace to the torn hearts gathered at that Mass.

—*Kara Werner*

In 1987, I was transferred through my job from Salt Lake City, Utah, to Houston, Texas. My husband had to stay in Salt Lake City to finish out his job, so our daughter, Santina, and I left ahead of him. A couple days after we got settled into our temporary living place, the first ordèr of business was to locate the nearest Catholic church. And so we found it, Saints Simon and Jude Catholic Parish.

I will never forget how it felt as we walked into the church. I had been filled with lots of anxiety and excitement from the move, getting Santina established in a new school, starting my new position at work, and of course, there was the culture shock! But as we entered the beautiful Catholic parish, I felt completely at home, and all my anxiety immediately melted away. I was at peace! Oh, what a wonderful gift it was. I knew God was with Santina and me and would take care of us, especially since my husband would not be joining us for about three months. As we sat in the pew, in the quiet, I remember thinking, "The Catholic Church is extraordinary, phenomenal, absolutely amazing! No matter what Catholic Church you visit in the entire world, *everything* remains the same: the altar, pews, Mass, rituals, priests, deacons, altar servers, warmth of the people. The love of Jesus shines through and is clearly evident. Wow!" Yes, we *are* one, holy, catholic, and apostolic faith; the one true Church, in which I am proud and blessed to belong.

—*Toni Hyler*

My favorite memory as a Catholic was when I was in seventh grade preparing for confirmation. We met as a class in the church hall once a week to hear the lesson from the teacher—who happened to be my mom (how embarrassing!). Our parish priest was there that day, and we were talking about the choice we were making to become full members of the Catholic Church.

As it was the beginning of Lent, my mom asked Father, "What are you giving up for Lent this year?"

Father said breezily (in front of all of us oh-so-cool teens), "Sex."

My mom and the other adults present burst out laughing, and all the kids in the room had eyes as big as dinner plates. I will never forget that day because it taught me that:

1. My mom knows the word *sex*—kill me now.
2. The priest has a sense of humor—who knew?
3. I actually enjoyed being at church and talking with these experienced Catholics.

It was so refreshing and fun! How amazing to feel as a young woman a sense of community beyond that of my immediate family.

—*Tanya Elliott*

I am not Catholic, but my twenty-six-year-old daughter converted to Catholicism during her sophomore year of high school. She has a strong faith and during high school participated in small groups and other activities at her parish. As an Anglican, I am comfortable attending Mass as easily as my church. About four years ago, my daughter introduced me to Dynamic Catholic. We were preparing for Lent, and she told me about the daily reading during Lent. Of course, I love the tagline, "Best Lent Ever." So that is where it began for me.

The daily reading is my morning devotion. I have a prayer card hung in my car, which is a great time for me to talk and listen to God. I share these cards with others. And, because the beauty and simplicity of Dynamic Catholic has touched me and my life, I feel what small amount I give just might further the cause. Oh, and all the materials you send to me I take to my daughter's Catholic high school, where they add the books and materials to the school's lending library.

—*Charlotte Ellington*

I have many memories in my short twenty-seven years of being Catholic, notwithstanding the first time I received Communion, but most recently our friends joined us on the Dynamic Catholic 2016 trip to Italy. My favorite Catholic memory now is renewing our marriage vows at the last Mass in Assisi. To have experienced Italy from a Catholic perspective and then to end on such a poignant note of renewal was a memory I will cherish for many years.

—*Olivia McCormick*

My most memorable moment as a Catholic was when I started to see how certain puzzle pieces fit together with other pieces in my life. One day as I was reflecting on my life, mainly my marriage, I saw how God's hand was involved in every aspect of my happiness. I saw how what I used to call luck could have changed many variables and the outcome of my life today. I remember thinking that this wasn't luck, that it had to have been the Holy Spirit guiding and reaffirming my choices early on in life.

I love that the focus of Mass is always on God. Others may say that Mass is boring, but I think the problem is that they make it about themselves and not God. I know some homilies are better than others, but yet God is always present regardless of the homily. Once I realized I was in his presence and that I could develop a relationship with him, I saw Mass in a different light. I began to grow in my Catholic faith, knowing that it is simple yet complex. It is simple in that you just have to go to Mass once a week and try to become the-best-version-of-yourself at your own speed and God will have mercy on you. Yet it is also complex because you can't ever satisfy that relationship with God. You are never done learning or doing things to become the-best-version-of-yourself. Being Catholic pushes us to continue to be the-best-version-of-ourselves over and over.

—*Patricia Baeza*

Until I was nine years old, we lived on a farm—about two to three miles from the nearest Catholic church. Every Sunday my Italian grandfather and I walked to Mass. It was during this formative time that I first developed my love of Catholicism. Hand in hand we walked, and in his broken English we talked about where we were going and the importance of the Mass. This basic memory has stayed with me for over sixty-five years, and I have continued this tradition with my own children and grandchildren.

—*Beverly Muresan*

In 1993 my husband wanted to know what I wanted for my twentieth wedding anniversary. He was asking nearly a year in advance thinking it was going to be a *really expensive* gift that would require him to save for at least a year. I thought for a moment and said, "Steve, I would really like for you to become Catholic." He replied, "No, no, I mean a *gift*. What do you want?" "That is what I want," I replied. "You have been going to Mass every Sunday since we started dating. You come to Eucharistic Adoration. You support our children in Catholic school. You support their Catholic youth groups. You are more Catholic than most Catholics I know." My husband said nothing. I was not hopeful, but I was prayerful.

Several weeks later, my husband came home and told me that he and a mutual friend had joined a bowling league. For once the Holy Spirit zipped my mouth tight, and I didn't say a word. (I'm a lawyer and I tend to talk a *lot* and say exactly what is on my mind.) I knew that friend needed my husband's time, but so did I. Our friend had been suicidal earlier that year and my husband had walked in on him and saved his life, so I didn't say a word. So, once a week I stayed home with the kids after working all day and supervised homework and baths, washed the youngest daughter's hair, and did all the other chores that I normally did, only I did it alone.

My husband wasn't very forthcoming about the bowling. The most I ever got when I inquired, "How was bowling tonight?" was "Fine." "It was interesting." "I had a lot of fun tonight." The answers were always vague. He would never tell me his bowling score or who was beating whom. I quit asking after a while. God only knew what he and our friend were really up to.

Nearly nine months later, on Holy Saturday, my cousin, who was a monsignor and the rector at the local seminary about twenty miles away, called and asked me how I would like to bring the children down to St. Bernard's Church in Fort Lauderdale, almost an hour away. In my head I was thinking, "Are you kidding me? Get four kids bathed, dressed for Easter Vigil Mass, and down to Fort Lauderdale in a couple hours?" Then he said, "You know how much St. Bernard's means to me, right?" "Oh, yes, I know. It was your dad's name and your first parish." Then, I couldn't believe it—I said, "Sure, we would love to come." Next thing you know I am pressing dresses, fixing hair, and getting kids ready for Mass, which we'd had zero intention of attending until Easter Sunday morning.

When I arrived, my cousin was waiting at the door. He said, "Peg, I've got a little problem here tonight, and I know you can fix it for me. Will you help me out?" (Did I mention that I *love* this priest who is my cousin?) "Sure. What do you need?" I thought for certain he was going to tell me he needed a lector, but he didn't. He said, "Peg, one of the candidates tonight doesn't have a sponsor, and I need you to step in and be his sponsor." I said, "Really? Come on, now. You are supposed to know this person, pray for this person, and help this person through RCIA. How am I going to be able to stand up for someone else?" The good monsignor said, "Don't worry about it. You'll do just fine." So I said, "Do you think I could at least meet this person BEFORE Mass starts?" Monsignor said, "Yes. You can. You know him quite well, as a matter of fact. He's standing right beside you." I looked to my left and there was no one. I looked to my right and there was my husband beaming with pride. I said, "You? You are going to become a Catholic tonight?" "Yes," my husband replied. I burst out crying. I had no idea that he and our friend had been taking RCIA down at the seminary each week. There was no bowling!

It is singularly the greatest Catholic memory I have to this day. Holy Saturday was April 2. My birthday was the following week. Not too shabby for a twentieth anniversary gift! BEST MEMORY EVER! BEST GIFT EVER!

—*Peggy Rowe-Linn*

It may sound strange, but the memories which are burned into my consciousness the most are Catholic funeral Masses. I feel sorry for the families when I go to secular "end of life" services. They skirt over the reality of what has happened. A loved one has finished the race and will be judged by Christ. The Catholic funeral Mass is so powerful to me. The entire ritual is an awesome prayer for the soul of the departed person. Both of my parents' funerals were so powerful. I could feel God's presence, and while it was emotionally difficult, it was also packed with joy, hope, and healing. Nobody pushes their members toward heaven at the end of their life like the Catholic Church!

—*Mark Taylor*

One of my favorite moments being a Catholic was having my parish pass out one of Matthew Kelly's CDs on the seven pillars; it changed my whole perspective on what being Catholic meant and gave me a new energy and determination to discover more about my faith.

—*Matt Scaring*

I'm going to share a recent memory. During Lent our church had Adoration every Friday morning. I spent one Friday morning in the presence of our Lord. I prayed so deeply, so strongly. I left around 10:45 a.m. I cannot begin to describe how

I felt the rest of the day. It was virtually as if every cell in my body was bursting with joy. I couldn't stop smiling. I felt this radiant, beautiful energy bubbling from inside. It remained so all day. I am generally a positive, happy person . . . but this was an energy and feeling that is hard to describe. I felt myself being extra patient with others, extra loving. What a gift! I can't wait until next Adoration!

—*Becky Boydston*

My favorite memory as a Catholic is going to Mass with my grandmother who had an incredible devotion to our Blessed Mother. I believe my grandmother was a saint among us, and I honor her by continuing her tradition of daily Mass and prayer.

—*Carla Mallory*

The first year we were married, my wife and I lived in a suburb of Washington, D.C. We had received some nice Lenox figurines for the start of a nativity set. My wife's father made a stable for us—it was nothing fancy, just some pieces of stained wood screwed together, but it meant so much to us because he was not a woodworker or a "crafty" type of person. We set up our nativity scene in our living room before Christmas, and carried on with our busy lives.

One Saturday, we were out running around, fighting the normal Christmas mobs while trying to get our holiday shopping done. When we came home early in the evening, exhausted from our busy day, we walked in the door and saw a single beam of light shining through the window, right on the baby Jesus. It stopped us dead in our tracks, reminding us what the season is really supposed to be all about.

—*Joe Miskey*

My best memory is midnight Mass on Christmas Eve with my family—in my Christmas pajamas. The subtle fragrance of the fresh-cut tree on the altar that housed the nativity, the dim lights throughout church with hundreds of candles dancing in the darkness, the hauntingly beautiful sounds of the choir are forever etched into my memory. I felt loved and protected.
—*Lori Loschiavo*

My ordination to the diaconate is my favorite memory as a Catholic. After five difficult years, all the study and sacrifice was worth it; to have my wife, my pastor, and my family there made it not just my best memory as a Catholic, but the greatest day in my life.
—*Gregory Ris*

When I was a little girl, one day my mother shared with me that she had planned on going into the convent. Instead she met my father, fell in love, and received the sacrament of marriage. I could not believe it. I asked her *why* in the world had she wanted to become a "nun"? Her answer shocked me. She said, "The sisters that I spent time with were the happiest people I had ever known. I love being a mother, but that was a very happy time for me. To this day, I have never known anyone happier." She spoke of how cheerful and kind the nuns were and how they were so happy serving others. I could not believe that someone could give up their life and be so happy. Years later, I do appreciate this story, and I make a point of sharing it with others. It is story that reminds me of how great our faith is and how we are called to serve *and* to be happy and cheerful while doing so. It is a cherished memory for me.
—*Jennifer Chiusano*

This is a hard question to answer but I truly believe it is that one confession, after my worst days, when I really knew God had forgiven me. (I am still working on doing the same for myself.)
—*Cathy Ludwick*

My favorite memory is the words of a tiny, old nun who taught us before we made our first Communion. She told us how very special that time is when we receive Jesus and go back to our pew and get to talk and be with him. She made me know that Jesus loves me and is really there. This was a very crucial time to know this, as my parents were having marital problems and would be separated one and a half years later. Her words have always been with me, especially when I have searched other Christian denominations, and they are truly the reason why I am still Catholic.
—*JoAnn Scholl*

My favorite memory as a Catholic is my homecoming. I was a non-practicing Catholic for about sixteen years after my confirmation. My husband and I only darkened church doors long enough to be married and have our children baptized. It took the crisis of nearly losing our marriage to bring us home. Somehow, instinctively, I knew that the institution that had sanctified our marriage was where we could find healing. It happened to be the first Sunday of Advent when I found myself home again. And what a homecoming it was! I think I cried for most of the Mass. The music ministry sounded like a choir of angels. God merely needs a crack in the door in order for his mercy to flood in. God blessed us with a more beautiful marriage than I could have ever envisioned when we walked down the aisle. Suffering endeared us to God. In his wisdom, he knew the bitterness of our suffering

would result in a marriage where he was finally welcomed to work his grace everywhere: around the family table, in the bedroom, and most importantly—in our hearts.
—*Julie Zasada*

My favorite memory as a Catholic was last year when my eight-year-old daughter made her first reconciliation. She wanted to be first in the confessional, and when she came out of the confessional, she was beaming. She was literally jumping up and down with a huge smile and so excited that she had a fresh start to do the right thing. I thought, if only we all could be that excited about going to confession, and afterward be excited enough to jump with joy!
—*Sally Blymyer*

My funniest memory is getting stuck in the confessional room after making my first reconciliation. I couldn't open the door, so went back and knelt on the cushion to ask for help. The priest started the whole intro again, thinking I was a new kid, at which point I started to yell very loudly. My mom, sitting outside, heard the commotion and with some help was able to open the *very sticky* door. We have had some good laughs over the years from that one! My best Mass attended was at the Basilica of Santa Maria Maggiore in Bergamo, Italy. I couldn't understand Italian, but the sheer magnificence and atmosphere in the church was incredible.
—*Bronny Bowman*

My favorite memory is going to confession in 2000. I told the priest I had not been to Mass since 1964. I expected him to faint,

but after a brief pause he asked me, "So what else is bothering you?" I have not been the same since.
—*Norman Cyr*

One of my favorite memories as a Catholic happened about seven years ago when I was praying in the Adoration chapel. Pin-drop silent, as you know. And I had just shared my desire with God to get to know his mother better. About fifteen seconds later, an entire men's Christ Renews His Parish (Welcome) retreat group walked into the Adoration chapel and started SINGING the rosary out loud. Talk about fast! Wow. And so very impactful! The Marian journey has continued, and God has been consistent in not being outdone in generosity. He has called me to a Marian apostolate that, as my co-founder and I like to say, is THE BEST GIG EVER.
—*Deanne Miller*

My favorite memory is the day my six-year-old grandson asked from the second pew in his Irish whisper, "Nana, why can't I go receive Communion? I already know its Jesus!" I told him, "Sheamus, you are light-years ahead of most people receiving Communion, but you will have to be patient!"
—*Kathleen Caruso*

My fondest memory of being Catholic was after a confession. My girlfriend saw me before and after, and she saw such a change in me that she became Catholic!
—*Chris Sprague*

I was a convert when I was twenty-one. It was a difficult decision but one I had been considering from the time I was sixteen. My family was Southern Baptist, and my grandfather was a deacon. I started attending Mass when I was eighteen, and I felt like I had found my home in life. When I was baptized, none of my family was present, but I knew I had made the right decision. My family eventually accepted my conversion. One day, some years later, my mother told me she respected me for my convictions and faith. I thanked God for the courage and tenacity to follow my heart.

—*Diane Fox*

There are so many good memories—it is very hard to choose just one. Throughout my life, God has been so kind and gracious to my family and me. He has always sent us good, loving, and faithful priests, who have visited us and who would spend Sundays at our house. We would have dinner and spend hours talking and learning and sharing stories. It is truly such a grace to have loving priests who are good shepherds!

—*Kathy Saba*

I have always liked the peace I felt after confession. I love that God is a God of second chances.

—*David Ebertowski*

I joined the Marine Corps at age seventeen and left my home for the first time when I was eighteen. I missed the comfort of my family, my neighborhood, my friends, and the routine of my life. When I attended Mass for the first time in the Marines, I realized that the Mass was the same everywhere, and that we are connected to each other around the world during the Mass—where heaven meets earth.

—*Matt Rieck*

My favorite memory of being Catholic is the funeral celebration of my nineteen-year-old son thirty years ago, when three priests co-celebrated his life to an overflowing congregation. They delivered the message that he would be able to touch so many more lives with his light from heaven than he could have on earth . . . This message meant the world to me.
—*Name Withheld*

My favorite memory as a Catholic came after the sacrament of reconciliation. This one particular time was so different and so beautiful because as I was listening to the priest speak, I actually "felt" forgiveness, "felt" the presence of Jesus in this priest, "felt" holiness like never before. I've known some holy people in my life and lived a few holy moments too, but nothing like what happened during this particular sacrament.
—*Marcia McMillen*

My favorite memories are the sacraments when I was growing up and, most recently, going on the Christ Renews His Parish (Welcome) retreat.
—*Dave Carlton*

My favorite memory as a Catholic was going to the Stations of the Cross. I went to a Catholic school for the first eight years of my schooling, and going to Stations during Lent was the norm. But when I was eighteen or nineteen, while reading one of the responses, it hit me that Jesus died for me. I had known that, but this time it *really* hit me, and I started to cry. I think that was the day the knowing in my head went into my heart. To this day that memory can bring me to tears—tears of joy.
—*Janet MacKeller*

My favorite memory of being a Catholic was in 2016 when I wrote my dad a letter personally inviting him to become a Catholic. I felt called to do so by God, and just responding to that call in and of itself is my favorite memory. I did not know what the outcome would be, but it filled me with joy to give personal testimony to my life as a Catholic. In the letter I thanked him for being a wonderful father and for everything he had done for me, including making it possible for me to attend a Catholic grade school and a Catholic high school. My dad grew up Lutheran and has gone to the Catholic church with my mom and me my entire life. We always went as a family together, which was great!

He responded so warmly and positively! He said he had always thought about becoming Catholic and knew that he would do it someday; he just was never sure of the right time.

Late in 2017, I got a call from my mom. She said my dad was thinking of attending an RCIA meeting that night, and she asked me to pray that he would have the courage to go.

Long story short, he went to the meeting, has been going to classes every week since, and became a Catholic at the Easter Vigil. As you can imagine, we are thrilled! God is good! I love that God gave me a small part in this wonderful part of my dad's life.

—*Jenny Wilson*

My best memory is when I discovered Dynamic Catholic three years ago. Even though I have always been Catholic, I didn't have the personal relationship with Jesus that I have now because of you.

—*Rose Reed*

I would have to say that my favorite memory was learning that my best childhood friend was going to enter the seminary. I remember how happy and excited he was, which in turn made me excited and happy. Watching him grow closer to God, I grew closer to God. He did become a priest, and just celebrated forty years as a priest. It has been so cool to see how his parishioners love him.

—*Joe Konecny*

My favorite memory as a Catholic is going to the cry room for lunch when I was in seventh grade to spend time by myself in earnest prayer. During that thirty minutes, I truly received the Holy Spirit.

—*Kristine Schaefer*

The greatest memory I have comes from the day I took my first temporary vows. In 1992, after my novitiate year, I was blessed to profess the evangelical councils of poverty, chastity, and obedience. I could write for hours about the afternoon of August 1, 1992, but to have the opportunity to follow great saints, great men who give of their lives, is the biggest blessing I could imagine.

—*Fr. Steve*

As the littlest child in my school, unfortunately I was picked on, and no one would play with me on the playground. Because I was Catholic, I would leave the playground and walk over to the church, where I found my *best* friend waiting for me there in the tabernacle. I would talk to Jesus and Mary and kneel before that tabernacle *knowing* that my Lord and my God, my best friend, was there to listen to me and love me. I used to ask him to just take me to heaven, as no one would mind. God knew the bigger plan, so he left me here. We are *still* best friends, and I *still* love visiting him in every tabernacle I can find, and especially in Adoration.

—*Rita Zimmerman*

My wife and I became legal guardians to a young boy who was faced with several big challenges in his life. One of the activities we involved him in was the faith formation program at our church. One evening we were invited along with the students to attend a talk by Fr. Donald Calloway. His talk was about his personal conversion, and he then went on to talk about "cafeteria Catholics." He did this in such a compassionate way, yet it pierced my heart and ego because I realized I was one of them. That began a search to find my "true" self and understand God's will for me. This is daily, moment-by-moment effort.

—*Tom Drapeau*

I have a lifetime of memories! One memory is finding Dynamic Catholic two years ago. I had just gone through some really tough surgeries and was feeling pretty low. A good friend of mine came to visit me and brought me a copy of *Rediscover Jesus*. She had just been to one of Matthew Kelly's talks and raved about him. I began reading and subscribing to the daily emails. My faith was lifted so much, and it got me through a tough health issue. Today I share these messages with my husband and children, especially at critical times in their lives.

—*Nancy Carney*

My husband and I were cradle Catholics, but we were only going through the motions. A few years ago we read Matthew Kelly's book *Rediscover Catholicism*, and this started a huge transformation in our faith. It led us to make our Cursillo weekend, which has been life-changing.

—*Christine Kirchoff*

I believe that God speaks to us all, but in different ways and at different times. I was living life as I always had—on my own terms. I was looking forward to my retirement from the teaching profession in June. I had all these big plans: I would travel, volunteer, spend time with my grandchildren, attend a Bible study with my sister, and get back into my church. (Did you notice the things that were at the end of my list of things to do?)

I was born and raised a Catholic, and my faith had gotten me through some pretty rough times in my life. I found that I could lean on it when I needed it but put it on the back burner when I didn't. My Catholic faith and relationship God were not in my whole heart and soul; one could definitely refer to me as a part-timer. In fact, up until that awful day when my world was turned upside down, I had been away from my parish for over two years. I had every good reason for not attending church—lesson plans needed to be done, grandchildren needed to be watched . . . you name it, I came up with it. Fortunately for me, God felt that I needed a wake-up call, and just like that it happened.

On March 17, 2017, I received the news that my thirty-eight-year-old son had died unexpectedly, leaving behind a wife and two young daughters to grieve his passing, along with a sister and brother-in-law, a brother and sister-in-law, many nieces and nephews, aunts, grandparents, and parents. I moved through the next couple of months as if in a fog, and some days I didn't think I was going to be able to make it, because, I realize now, I was trying to do it on my own.

On this one particularly rough night as I lay in bed sobbing to my husband that I couldn't go on any longer, I briefly opened my eyes to see he was praying over me. I quickly closed them again and just let him continue. It was at this very moment that I felt a peace descend upon me. It was like Jesus laid a warm blanket of comfort over me. It was then I knew I would not have to travel this road alone, and that when I needed him most, he would be there to hold me up. I began my journey back into the Catholic Church and the faith that had sustained me so many times before. Only this time, it would not be on my terms, but all for his glory. On several occasions since that fateful night, he has let me know that he is still here, guiding me and watching over me.

—*Erin Bozeman*

My favorite memory as a Catholic is attending my diocesan youth summer camp. Those days by the lake, in the company of other lively, happy, and spiritually energized young people, were some of the best days of my life. I remember one day laughing so hard I genuinely thought I was going to throw up, and thinking that this must just be the height of delirious joy. I had had a sense of God from a young age, and I had always been attracted to Christianity's call to love and service, but I had been a bit suspicious of the more formal aspects of the Catholic faith—the liturgy, the sacraments, and especially some of the moral "rules." But when I was sixteen, the counselors of that camp sat me down and taught me about the theology of the body, and it blew my mind. They quickly dismantled so many of our culture's lies about the meaning of sexuality, and they offered me a substantial and attractive alternative. I couldn't believe what I was hearing. Everyone I had met previously (Catholics included) had taken it as a given that the Church didn't know what she was talking about when it came to sexuality, and that Catholicism's teachings on sex were a bunch of nos. But this was so *positive* and so compelling. From that experience on, I trusted the Church, and I began to see that all of the things I hadn't quite accepted were legitimate and true. Catholicism was something I could embrace wholeheartedly! I gave my heart to it fully and haven't looked back, and while at times it's been a wild ride, I count my Catholic faith as the single greatest gift of my life.

—*Name Withheld*

My favorite memory is when both my husband and I went to a Christ Renews His Parish (Welcome) weekend. This put so many unanswered questions about our religion and faith in perspective—it was an unbelievable feeling that I'd never had before.

From that experience we began having weekly Bible meetings with a number of people we met from our church. What a wonderful feeling to have them enter our home with the Bible on our coffee table and three candles lit. The glow of the candles brought a sense of serenity to the room . . . Jesus was there with all of us.

—*Corrine Lewis*

When I was a little girl, our neighborhood church was the only place in the world that I felt safe from all the things that were happening in my life. The protection of our Holy Mother always made me feel safe. Fortunately, in those days, churches had the holy rosary every evening in May and October, and that was the only time my father would let me leave the house. I am seventy years old now, and I will remember that feeling for the rest of my life.

—*Marie Hurley*

This may sound strange, but what should have been a scary and awful experience has turned into one of the most wonderful experiences of my life! When my middle daughter was hanging on to life by a thread, I turned to Jesus and Mary like never before. I remember placing my daughter in the arms of Mary and asking Jesus to hold her hand. My husband and I sought reconciliation because we knew we wanted nothing to block our prayers, and over the next month we experienced our own prayer and those of so many others . . . That month of ICU was so grace-filled! One of the doctors came in one day and said, "I have never walked into an ICU room before and felt such peace!" This would not have been possible without my Catholic faith!

—*Missy Hail*

My husband and I have never left the Church, but we came close after attending a Bible study with my brother (who had left) and a group of Evangelicals. When challenged with tough questions, we went to our priest, who hooked us up with our pastoral associate. He answered questions beyond those questions, and we came to know our faith and ultimately fall in love with the Catholic Church for the first time. Our favorite memory is when we truly became Catholic: heart, mind, and soul.

—*Louise Gillmore*

My favorite memory is the two years I spent in a Franciscan seminary. While it turned out that was not my vocation, I will always remember that time with great fondness. It was a major part of my maturation as an adult.

—*Peter England*

My husband and I just had our marriage convalidated four years ago during a Mass. To finally be "all in" as a Catholic was and is a beautiful place to be. For so many years we were Catholic by our rules, and now we are finally home!

—*Jo Brennan*

When I was a young teen, I had the opportunity to get to know our priest, Fr. "Bud" Wiesler, at our small church in rural Tubac, Arizona, when I volunteered to do some of the readings during Mass. He later asked me if I would serve at the altar, and I said yes. He was a very gentle man, and his instructions were the simplest of simple: "When I point to something, please hand it to me." Fr. Bud would share little bits of wisdom with me in the sacristy before Mass too. I remember him saying, for instance, "Always give thanks to God. He likes hearing when we're thankful."

Fr. Bud was later reassigned, and in 2003 we heard he had passed. My mother and I attended his funeral and were amazed to see the number of people there. Our small rural church maybe held 120 people max, but there were easily four or five times that many people in attendance. We heard that Fr. Bud had given all of his small salary to help the poor; he also used to walk the streets in the evening, ministering to the people he found.

I felt so proud to have known such a holy man. He told me about and modeled God's love for me.

—*Michael O'Keefe*

A couple of years after teaching PSR (Parish School of Religion), one of my former students was seriously injured in an ATV accident, and at first he was given only hours to live. Then he was expected to be a quadriplegic. Next he was certain to have severe brain damage. The Sisters of Mercy prayed over him at the hospital with his family. Thirty days later he walked out of the hospital as if nothing had happened. I had witnessed a miracle. If ever there was a doubt in my little brain, it didn't exist after that.
—*John Drabik*

I am a cradle Catholic and was raised by strict parents, and we never missed a Sunday Mass. However, when I was young I did not have a complete understanding of the importance of the Mass and our wonderful Lord. There was so much that I did not know. After I got married, I fell away from the Church because of my lack of religious education, and my husband did not believe either. Without a strong support system, I did not have the inner strength to go back to church on my own.

In 2001, at the age of forty, I was invited to a Christ Renews His Parish (Welcome) weekend at a local parish. Words cannot describe the power of the weekend and how it transformed my life . . . To this day I remember every detail of this amazing experience. After that weekend, I was given the strength by our beautiful Jesus Christ to leave an abusive relationship, I became an active parishioner in my church, I have brought non-believers back to the Church through my beliefs and faith, I serve the poor and the dying, and I've recently experienced a miracle; this all came about because of the love of our beautiful Jesus Christ.
—*Toni Brady*

My greatest memory is when I made a general confession after having been living in a state of mortal sin for many years. To know I had sanctifying grace in my soul was a beautiful thing!
—*Shawn Kovash*

I was in Japan for a while and circumstances made me give up on finding a nearby church. I really missed Mass, and I went out for a walk and shared that thought with God. Within minutes I walked right by a Catholic church where Mass was beginning in five minutes. God is good! I felt so at home and welcome, even though the reserved Japanese barely acknowledged me. Of course the sign of peace was a quiet bow instead of a handshake. It was one of my favorite memories of Mass.
—*Angela Lennox*

We were in France on a bus tour when 9/11 happened. The next night we went to the evening rosary recitation in Lourdes. It was amazing! It was so crowded, we could barely move, but everyone seemed to be comfortable. Thousands of people, praying in hundreds of different languages, all praying for the same thing: peace. This was the Catholic faith in action, and it was alive!
—*June Andrews*

My favorite memory is the first time I attended Adoration. It overwhelmed me with a sense of peace and gave me a quiet mind.
—*Paul Thibeault*

I am attending RCIA to learn more about my beautiful religion,

and at age eighty-seven, I'm receiving so many wonderful answers to some of the questions I have struggled with.
—*Jean Woytek*

My favorite memory as a Catholic is the first time I heard a Catholic priest talk about having a relationship with Jesus Christ. I was blown away, because I'd never heard a Catholic priest say that in a homily before. It seemed to be something only Protestants talked about. I knew that something big was happening in our Catholic religion. God's Holy Spirit was awakening souls!
—*Deb Chmelar*

One of my favorite memories as a Catholic was when I was twelve years old. My mom was in the hospital battling leukemia. We went to see her on the weekends. One Sunday at the hospital I stayed with her after everybody else had left. One of the chaplains came in and gave my mom Holy Communion. She had been in a lot of pain that day. When she received Communion, a real peace came over her, and she began to glow. Right then and there I knew the Eucharist was real. I knew that I would never leave the Eucharist.
—*Lynn Adelman*

My favorite moment being a Catholic was walking through the doors of the church to have my twin sons baptized. I was profoundly aware that they were a gift from God and I was returning them to him to say thank you, to commit them to his care, and to commit myself to bringing them up to know God and to be godly men.
—*Carole Ambroziak*

Although I have many wonderful memories relating to the Catholic Church, there is one that has been a truly magnificent experience for me. In 2015 I was the winner of a pilgrimage to Italy with Dynamic Catholic. My wife, Carla, and I had always dreamed of going on a pilgrimage to Italy, but as a retired firefighter, it was just a little beyond our means. You cannot imagine our joy when we received the news that I was a winner. I was someone who, other than my lovely wife's hand in marriage, had never won anything of significance in my entire life! With my trip paid for, we could both afford to go on a pilgrimage that previously we had only been able to dream about. It was a truly wonderful and life-changing experience for both of us. To be able to visit Rome, see the Holy Father in person, attend Mass in St Peter's Basilica, and tour the Basilica and the Vatican museum was a dream come true. Monte Cassino, San Giovanni Rotondo, Lanciano, Assisi, Matthew Kelly, Dr. Allen Hunt, Monsignor Lisante, Father Sherry, Father Deiters, the members from Dynamic Catholic, 206 Tours and all of the members of our pilgrimage group made for an unforgettable and blessed experience. We were truly blessed!

—*Thomas Sullivan*

I treasure the memory of our family gathering to say the rosary together. Now we all do the rosary every Wednesday as a family (we do a virtual rosary because we are spread across Massachusetts, New Jersey, Connecticut, Virginia, and California). We rotate the intentions—each sibling gets a week of their intention—and that's what we all pray for.

—*Name Withheld*

Favorite memory: the moment my wife and I found each other in the back of a confession line a few years after we were both widowed.
—*Peter Korman*

By far, the single most treasured memory of my Catholic faith is praying the rosary as a family. We used the scriptural rosary, and the stories of Jesus' life made a deep and lasting impact on me. I can still see my father's face when we were done. He'd light up with this profound joy and say something like, "Okay, wonderful!" I would always watch for his reaction because it was so infectious.
—*Name Withheld*

I worked as a parish secretary for three years. I loved being involved with and immersed in all the activities of a Catholic parish, supporting the parish priests, and hearing about all the activities going on in the diocese.
—*Annie Chermak*

I was in a really dark place. I had no hope. I had tried to end my life. I found a therapist, and I was on medication, but nothing had changed. I had no reason to live. My friend called and told me that he was giving me a scholarship to an ACTS retreat. I gave him every excuse in the book, but the Holy Spirit had other plans for me. I went on the retreat. I had a renewal in my faith. I found a new and real relationship with Jesus Christ. I also found my reason to live; this was God's plan for me. My retreat was in 2011, and I have been 100 percent involved in the ACTS program ever since. Thanks to ACTS, I have a real "family," I have a purpose, I have joined many other volunteer groups through the ACTS community, and I have faith, hope, and love in God, in Jesus Christ, in the Holy Spirit, and in my neighbor.

—*Elsa Marsh*

My favorite memory is my personal conversion story. My senior year of high school, I wanted to make the state championships for swimming. Reading Mark 11:24, I knew God would provide whatever I asked for in prayer and believed I would receive. I prayed the rosary each day in addition to swimming four hours a day, and God helped me visualize and achieve my goal of making the state championships! From that moment, any time temptation or doubts started to form in my mind, I would think back to this favorite memory, and my faith would be strengthened as a Catholic.

—*Michael Phinney*

My favorite memory is of my mother teaching me to pray when I was about five years old. I would pray that God would not let me fall asleep until I said my prayers. I have distinct memories of nights when I was six or seven, tossing and turning until I remembered to pray. Then, like Peter, James, and John, I couldn't stay awake once I began to pray!

—*Bill O'Brien*

My favorite memory is the day my life changed in Adoration when I came before the Lord as a desperate sinner and he comforted me. Jesus revealed to me that he understood my loneliness

and pain because he had experienced the same thing in the garden before he was arrested to be crucified. Because of this I knew
I was not alone, and my life changed forever. I was brought out of
the depths of despair, and slowly over time I was freed from the
habitual sin I had been a slave to.
—*Erika Walker*

My family was going through turmoil—my brother and I both had
polio. My brother was seriously affected to where my mother had
to be away with him at different hospitals and rehab centers for
days and even weeks. The Sisters of St. Joseph from the elementary school would take me in, and my job was to polish the floors
around the altar, which I felt so very honored to do. I also found
where the "injured" statues were tucked away. I used to go to visit
them and "fix" them up and pray for them and ask them to pray
for me. I am sure they felt as abandoned as I did at that time. If I
could have, I would have slept with them to keep them company.
—*Stella Miller*

I went on a retreat my freshman year of high school. On that
retreat I heard the Gospel message for the first time. I learned
that God loved me personally and desired a personal relationship with me. There was confession and Adoration during Saturday night of the retreat. After going to confession and receiving
God's unconditional love and mercy, I knelt before the Eucharist.
Looking up at the Host I encountered a peace and joy I'd never
experienced before. At that moment I knew that Jesus loved me
personally, and desired to have a relationship with me.
—*Michael Jacobs*

I live in Maryland. In 1985 Pope John Paul II celebrated Mass at our baseball stadium (Camden Yards). My family (my husband and four very young children at that time) was honored to be asked, along with a senior couple, to carry up the offertory gifts. There was a rehearsal two days before the Mass at the stadium. As we rehearsed, there was all kinds of activity taking place there. The altar was still being constructed. Different things were being carried in and carried out, and rehearsals for other parts of the Mass and the day's celebrations were taking place. The scene was somewhat chaotic. I couldn't imagine how all of this was going to come together in time for Mass. But it did! And when I walked out onto the field that day, Camden Yards was no longer a baseball stadium. It was a church. Over fifty thousand people were gathered there to hear the proclaimed Word of God, receive the Holy Eucharist, and then be sent to proclaim the Good News! For the first time, I really understood that the Church is not a building. It is the people!

—*Karen Spivey*

My favorite memory as a Catholic is attending Mass with my family as a small child. My mother struggled with mental illness, and my father, although very hardworking, was emotionally absent, quiet, and hard to relate to. However, when we went to Mass, I got to see them at their best! My mother, who was often quick-tempered and emotionally unstable, would relax and be at peace. She would treat each of the four of us kids with tenderness and affection and would often rub my back or play with my hair as we listened to the readings. My father's love for the Lord would come forth, and he'd hold me in his arms with my head resting upon him in such a way that I could hear his voice vibrating in his chest as he sang. My parents were the-best-version-of-themselves at Mass, and as a result whenever I walk into a Catholic Church I feel like I'm home.

—*Lisa Pitkin*

My story would not have been possible without God rescuing me and showing me what was most important in my life, which led to my conversion to the Catholic faith in 1965 at the age of twenty-nine. My increased faith raised my spiritual life to new heights of talents and skills I'd never imagined. God gave me many challenges to test and prove my worth. I surrendered to many of God's graces, and my faith grew steadily in knowledge and understanding. I advanced significantly in stewardship and responsibilities for the benefit of my family and my work. I've felt most alive giving myself to an important purpose higher than myself—the love of the Catholic faith and doing God's will, which is discovering the-best-version-of-myself.

—*Jim Coleman*

After having a powerful experience at a weekend church retreat, nothing was ever the same again for me. I was determined not to forget that experience and not to slip back into old habits and patterns. I wanted to live my life in a way that reflected the great gift I had been given. I started attending Mass daily and spending time in conversational prayer with God throughout the day. I craved Scripture as if it were the most decadent of desserts. My appetite for it was insatiable. They say that when the student is ready, the teacher appears. I was ready, and for the first time in my life, the words on the page came alive. I read story after story of other sinners just like me, sinners who had a profound change of heart once they encountered God in the flesh. The God of all creation was talking to me, and I was listening.

I read in Paul's Letter to the Ephesians, "For by grace you have been saved through faith, and this is not from you; it is the gift of God" (Ephesians 2:8). I got that! I was becoming increasingly aware of the magnitude of this gift I had been given. I had done nothing to earn this newfound faith. It was pure gift, and I most certainly did not deserve it. That's what made it grace, and I treasured it more than I have ever cherished anything in my life. In the past, I was waiting for God to track me down, but now, I was taking the initiative. I was pursuing God. I was cooperating with, rather than resisting, the work of his grace in my life.

In addition to Mass and Scripture, I was also drawn to the sacrament of reconciliation frequently. I know it's a Catholic "thing," and people joke all the time about "Catholic guilt," but there *is* something to speaking your transgressions aloud and hearing someone else say to you, "Your sins are forgiven." It was cathartic for me, and for the first time in my life, I wasn't going to reconciliation because I felt like I *had* to, I was going because I *wanted* to. I was keenly aware of my sinfulness, and I longed for forgiveness. I felt compelled to reflect on and examine my past with a fine-tooth comb, returning time and time again to confess sins I had long since forgotten about. There were many things that I kept dredging up, things I really struggled to let go of. Finally, one day, after going several times in a period of only a few weeks, my priest said, "Bo, I really believe that God wants you to stop looking back and move forward."

I tried, but there was one more blemish in my past that gradually came into glaring relief. Three years earlier, I'd had a vasectomy. At the time, I certainly didn't think it had anything to do with my faith or my relationship with God. For me, it was a matter of practicality. Stacy and I got married and started having children when we were very young, still in college. For me, I saw the vasectomy as my chance to "catch up" in my career and make up for lost time. Anxious to move on to the next stage of our lives, as soon as our third child, Nicky, was born, I started bugging Stacy about when I could have a vasectomy. She dismissed me, saying that I could do it once I turned thirty.

A month and a half after my thirtieth birthday, I took care of it and never looked back, that is, until three years later when everything changed. I had changed, and as God was molding and shaping my heart, my perceptions of my own sinful behavior were changing, as well as my understanding of my faith and the Church's teachings. I was starting to see God as the loving Creator of the universe, constantly giving birth to and sustaining life. I had never thought about that before. I was also starting to embrace my role as a co-creator, and that blew me away. God allowed us to bring life into this world as his partners. My sin was not trusting him in that partnership, and I knew I had to return to reconciliation.

What the priest said to me changed the course of my life and my family's life from that point forward. Hearing the regret in my voice, he said, "You know, Bo, when you walk out of here, you are forgiven, but . . . it sounds like it would be a great gift to your wife, and I know it would be an even greater gift to God as well, if you had it reversed." Immediately I knew in my heart what I needed to do. When I told Stacy, quiet tears streamed down her face, and she said, "Bo, I never wanted you to get the vasectomy in the first place."

Excited about the prospect of a vasectomy reversal, after doing some research, we found a doctor in San Antonio who performed reversals for half the price, so Stacy and I headed to Texas. It was an awesome experience. I had heard people talk about "joy," but I don't think I ever really understood what it meant to feel joy until this experience. Heading home with Stacy, I *knew* I felt true joy. I kept recalling two scenes from Scripture, Jesus' baptism and his Transfiguration. Both times, God's audible voice is heard saying to Jesus, "This is my beloved son in whom I am well pleased." That is exactly what I felt like God was saying to me and how he felt about me. *I* was his beloved son, and he was pleased with *me*!
—*Bo Govea*

Three

As a Catholic, What Are Your Hopes for the Future?

My hope for the future is that people will rediscover the Catholic faith and there will be "standing room only" at Sunday Mass again!
—*Mary Anne Linsell*

As a Catholic, my hope for the future is that all parents will understand their responsibility for teaching their children the principles of our faith. I hope they will focus on the future world that their children will have an impact on, and realize that teaching them to live their lives as true disciples of Christ will help ensure a world that God intended us to have.
—*Bruce Robertson*

My hope for the future is that we get back together as one nation under God.
—*Jim Mall*

My hope for future Catholics is that they find time to study the Bible more and reflect on what they are reading and learning. I have participated in many Bible studies, and I've found that other non-Catholic Christians know the Word of God in a different way than I do. As a Catholic I find that I get so caught up in rituals that I don't always process God's Word as I should. Don't get me wrong! I enjoy the rituals, but I have allowed them to be the only focus. I now have a dual focus during Mass: the Word of God and the rituals attached to the Mass.

—*Susan Wood*

My hope for the future is that the current movement toward secularism in our society is rapidly overturned . . . as a result of dynamic Catholicism and dynamic Christianity. I hope that people who have turned to everything except Jesus Christ to fill their emptiness finally find fulfillment and peace in him.

I want to see churches filled with families young and old, with friends who attend together, with groups of young people and young adults, with singles, with people from all walks of life, and with the elderly who have attended Mass all their lives.

I want to live in a world where society and world leaders are not afraid to talk about Christianity! To make BOLD statements about Christianity. To return to prayer in schools and before athletic events without discrimination against Christians. I want to live in a world that respects life, especially lives of the unborn.

I refuse to think, like so many pessimists say, that the Church is dying. Not if we can help it! Why do I KNOW this can all be done? Because I see people like Matthew Kelly—an individual who was inspired by a wonderful mentor—building a powerful organization with the mission to make the Catholic Church dynamic

and passionate again. To think that *one person* can effect that much change in our Church and daily spiritual lives in a relatively short time gives me total confidence that we will revive and thrive. . . .
—*Ann Molteni Bridenstine*

I hope that in the future our society and in particular kids think it is "cool" to be Catholic. That we (and in particular kids and teenagers) are not only proud to be Catholic but show our pride. You often see people wearing shirts, hats, etc. of a favorite team or college. People are proud of their teams and schools and love to show their pride. In high school it may be "cool" to be on a sports team or part of a certain activity. I dream of the day where my children (and one day grandchildren) are proud to be Catholic and want others to know they are Catholic. I dream of the day when the "cool kids" at school are the ones that are part of the Catholic youth group and other kids want to join the group. I dream of the day where Catholics as a whole are so proud of our faith that we want everyone to know that we are Catholic and what that really means. Cool to be Catholic!
—*Eric Knachel*

My hope for the future is for PEACE in the world, PEACE in our country, PEACE in our communities, PEACE in our families, and PEACE in each of our hearts.
—*Margaret Mueller*

My dreams for the Catholic Church are that:

1. Every Catholic would believe in the real presence of Jesus Christ in the Eucharist

2. Every Catholic would learn about and embrace what the Catholic Church has done for education and healthcare in the world

3. Every Catholic would be able and willing to defend their faith when others misrepresent what we do (and don't do)

4. Every Catholic would be a living sacrament—an outward sign of Jesus Christ in our troubled world.

—Gretchen Cooney

My hope for the future is that we all see that Jesus is the answer to all our prayers.

—Maria Sotelo

My hopes for Catholicism reside in the youth of today—that they would realize the beauty and importance of living our faith each day.

—Suzanne Muzzarelli

A strong vibrant Church for our precious grandchildren!

—Junnie Winters

My hope for the Catholic Church is that we inspire our young to make Mass and their faith a priority. So much of what they are going through can be positively reinforced at Mass. We must lead by example and show our younger generation all the blessings that come from making our faith an integral part of our life.

—Angie Gould-Wilmington

My hope for the future is that the Catholic Church will remain steadfast in upholding the moral tenets which are the foundation of our Christianity. So much of our moral fabric is eroding in the secular culture of today. If our Church cannot remain steadfast, where in the world will our culture be?

—*Janet Cook*

Several times in the last few years, I have watched my two teenage grandsons, along with several busloads of other teenagers, return from the March for Life and from the Steubenville retreat weekends.

They return tired from a long bus trip, but full of life and with hearts on fire for the Lord. I pray that they keep this fire burning in their hearts as they become adult Catholics. I believe they can bring this fire to their parishes and enlighten their parishes so that they realize what a strong light Jesus can bring to them. I am confident that this group will provide some priests for our future and many other active Catholic parishioners.

Many people give up on our youth, but I know they will bring life to their parishes. I trust that they will bring this fire for Jesus to the Church.

—*Jane Varick*

I hope for a Church refreshed, renewed, and strengthened by the trials she faces today.

—*Pamela Kavanaugh*

"That they may be one, as we are one" (John 17:22). My hope is that one day the rich praise and worship of our Protestant brothers and sisters will be fully reunited with the sacraments of the Catholic Church. For now, may we celebrate the truths we hold in common and prayerfully explore our reunion.

—*Nancy Bricker*

What is my future hope as a Catholic? My immediate response to this question is for the conversion of my family—my spouse and three adult children. I pray to Saint Monica on a daily basis for their conversion. I know God hears my prayers, and I see evidence of him working in their lives every day.

From a broader perspective, my hope as a Catholic is that all Catholics seek a deeper relationship with our Lord through the treasures of our faith and that Catholics who have discovered these treasures "be not afraid" of sharing these gifts with everyone they meet. Finally, my hope is that Catholics become missionary disciples of Christ by striving to be Jesus' hands and feet in a world in desperate need of a savior.

—*Lynn Marion*

My hope as a parent is that my children love God as much as I love him, and that my faith may be their faith when they reach adulthood and be passed on to their children.

—*Marieli Amador*

I hope and pray that once again society will turn away from relativism. It breaks my heart that preference has replaced Christian morality. It is everywhere, including my own family. So many people are afraid to speak how they really feel about their Catholic faith for fear of being shunned. It's not always easy to be a Catholic, but so worth it! I do struggle myself, but I am so grateful for Dynamic Catholic, who helps me return to what I have been taught and believe in. As I was doing "Best Lent Ever," I was struggling with some things that were happening at work. I was becoming very distraught and felt there was no light at the end of the tunnel. Then one day the light turned on when Matthew Kelly made a simple statement: "Just do the right thing." This impacted me so intensely, and I try to share this message with all I am able to. As a mother to two young adults who are subjected to all the relativism that is around, it is very challenging. I am grateful and blessed to have a husband who has worked side by side with me to share our faith, and hopefully by our example they will see what it means to be a faithful Catholic. Just as my almost-ninety-year-old mother continues to pray for her children, I too will continue to pray for my children and continue to grow in my faith.

—*Bernadine Smalley*

The Catholic Church is such a powerful influence for so many people. I would like to see more laypeople taking the active role of becoming deacons. I would also like to see the role of deacons expanded within the Church. I would like to see the Dynamic Catholic ministry expand in the US.

—*Lynn Bustos*

My hope is that we will see increased vocations to the priesthood and strong growth in the Catholic Church.

—*Donald Schade*

That more will return and embrace the Church and bring others to see the awesomeness of Catholicism!

—*Ceci Matthews*

My hope for the future is for something to sustain marriages, because in order to keep the families together we have to keep the marriages together. Families that pray together stay together.
—*Debbie Perez*

I hope more people know the genius of Catholicism and the young people come back!
—*Mary Beth Atherton*

I hope for my kids to inherit a love for the Church. It is my greatest goal as a parent to give them this treasure, our faith. I hope for good leaders and for freedom to worship.
—*Heather Tomas*

That all mankind will come to know Jesus in the breaking of the bread through our prayers, the examples we set, and our charity and love toward all.
—*Helen Lehner*

My hopes for the future include a more unified Catholic Church based on the sacred teachings of the magisterium and families actively supporting vocations for more priests and religious!
—*Mike Eikenberry*

My ultimate hope is that all Christians can come together to stand together as Team Christ and have one truly universal Church.
—*Vicki Faber*

Raising Catholic children and renewing the face of the earth one

person at a time, by radiating our love for our faith.
—*Kristen Ryan*

That the whole world—every nation, race, and current religious affiliation—convert to Catholicism. (Not too small a wish, right?)
—*Barbara Brady*

My hope for the future is that we find ways to revitalize Catholics as I have been revitalized. We have an amazing faith, it has an amazing history, and although our Church has had its questionable moments, it has withstood time and continued on.
—*Gigi McKinzie*

My hopes are to become a saint and help those around me to do the same.
—*Bill Moran*

I hope that we are able to be relevant. We need to be able to stay true to our fundamental Catholic beliefs but be willing to change in other ways to adapt to our current time.
—*Sue Janowski*

My hope for the future is to see the RCIA program grow in attendees so that each parish would need several teams to accommodate all those choosing to be active Catholics, and that this would happen because of what existing Catholics are doing to bring them in.
—*Ruth Munger*

My hope for the future is that every Catholic rises up and defends life from conception to death.
—*Annette Shaughnessy*

My hope for the future is for all Catholics, practicing and non-practicing, to truly learn the beauty of the Catholic faith by coming to know the Holy Spirit and allowing him to work in their lives.
—*Name Withheld*

It is my hope as a Catholic that we will see, in our lifetime, a reunification of Christians all over the world. That the rest of the Christian world will understand, FINALLY, that Jesus is the bridegroom and the Church is his bride, and that all of our "rules and regulations" are only meant to set us free from sin and set us on a path to eternal life.
—*Jim Furto*

I hope that Catholicism is rejuvenated and that people see that this great tradition has so much truth to it. In this world where people are starting to "create their own truths," I pray that once they begin to feel the emptiness that will come from that way of thinking, it will cause them to seek what will actually fill the emptiness, and that is the genius that is Catholicism.
—*Michelle Hurley*

My hope for the Church is that it will grow in numbers and unity and always listen to the Holy Spirit for guidance.
—*Kathy Sechler*

That our country's values move to reflect the two basic com-
mandments: love God and love one another!
—*Mike Caza*

My hope for the Catholic Church is that it can reach as many
people as possible to share its beauty. My hope is also that
we grow in Bible studies. We need to know the Bible. Read
it. Make notes in it. Memorize favorite Scriptures. Share *good*
experiences with others about Catholicism. I want the Church
to help its members to continue to grow in faith throughout
life.
—*Robin Emmons*

My hope for the future is that these churches would fill up once
again with our children and their children, worshipping in a
joyful manner, eager to be there. I hope we live our faith in a
more authentic manner, and that God becomes prominent in our
society, homes, and families once again.
—*Jean Pendleton*

My hope for the future is that Catholics in America and around
the world realize they need the Church for its wisdom, guidance,
and truth, and that living out the principles of Catholicism is the
best way to live.
—*Anthony Swierzbinski*

I hope that more lost sheep will come back to the Church—or just
come period!
—*Fr. Shaun Foggo*

As a Catholic, my hope for the future is the conversion of the world one person at a time as we grow in our faith and knowledge of God and his Church through intercessory prayer and awesome teachers like those at Dynamic Catholic. I desire to be a-better-version-of-myself every day. Be bold. Be Catholic.
—*Kathy Rodamaker*

We must find a way to invigorate the group of Catholics that just come to Mass but otherwise aren't involved. We also must become more active in bring back those who have fallen away from the Church, which unfortunately includes our children. We must be more active evangelists.
—*Jim Cannon*

My hope is that all Catholics learn and live their faith authentically.
—*Steve Wytrykusz*

I hope that the Catholic Church will develop more of a sense of community like I see in our Protestant brothers and sisters.
—*Sharon Squires*

My hope is that the Catholic Church will be reenergized, that both the clergy and laypeople will become the-best-version-of-themselves. As the media and people in general in the Western world become more secular, I hope that the Church can be a beacon of light for all.
—*John and Mary Ann Sorci*

My hope for the future is that prayer can be a part of every day in school. I hope abortion will come to an end. I pray for people to

find their happiness, their hopes and their dreams without crush-
ing someone else's. I hope for a world that makes choices based
on what Jesus would do rather than what a political group thinks
they should do. I hope for a future where people are content with
what they have and the life they are living because they recognize
that all they are and all they have comes from God.
—*Melanie Edmonson*

I pray daily that people begin to love and respect themselves and
others. I hope that the "veneer society" that we live in today begins to realize it isn't all about me, or my kids, or my little world. I
hope we love and respect each other and that these principles are
carried out in our daily words and actions, whether we are an important government official or the gardener in Bakersfield who is
trying to make a living. And I hope that all Catholic parents raise
their children to be knowledgeable in our faith by being good
role models and deepening their own faith.
—*Jo Ellen Mosher*

To see the Church rise up and be that beacon to minister to hurt
people. Our society is so lost and seeking the truths that the
Church teaches. The Church has been labeled as "out-of-date,"
"boring," and "an abusive institution," and it is hard to get society to
take the Church seriously anymore. My hope is that we can reach
out to touch people that need healing, to be the leader in healing,
education, assisting the poor, and safeguarding the vulnerable.
—*Carla Dill*

My deepest desire and hope for the future is for the conversion
of hearts to Jesus! I have started to say a daily novena for this re-

quest. For all peoples of the world to turn away from hate, mean-
ness, war, and violence and embrace love, kindness, compassion,
and peace! I pray for my husband, daughter, family members, and
friends that they will conscientiously choose to have God in their
daily lives—embracing him every day! Not only when things go
wrong, but be in relationship with him in all things!
—*Barbara Moore*

That the rosary becomes a worldwide means of praying.
—*Gloria Walker*

My hope for the future of Catholicism is that we in the boat will
not look down upon the roaring waves trying to capsize us, but
steadfastly keep our eyes on the Lord, strengthened by the Eucharist and the rosary.
—*Dorothy Rodgers*

My hopes for the future are great! When I look at the kids I teach
in high school religious education or my own kids, I see brightness out there. I hear the Holy Father's messages, tweets, and vid-
eos, and I know others like me can see the brightness at the end of
the darkness. My hopes fall to the concept that the youth of today
see the good examples of adults and emulate them. We should
have grand hopes—they *will* come to pass.
—*Brendan Bagley*

My hope for the future is that everyone can experience God's
love on a personal level.
—*James Conner*

My hope as a Catholic for the future is that we appreciate the importance of emulating Christ in everything we do. In so doing we will send a powerful evangelizing message that will bring people to Christ. Eliminating corruption and lack of Christian behavior on the part of Catholic leadership would dramatically increase Catholic influence in bringing people to the Church and therefore Christ.

—*Fred Stransky*

My hope is that all Catholics will give up trying to make their own decisions and pray for the Holy Spirit to guide them. I pray that we will look at Sundays and holy days not as days of obligation but as holy days of opportunity!

—*Michael Giobbi*

My hope for the future is that we can grow as a Church in being better disciples, better evangelists, better servants, better lovers, and better prayers.

—*James Smrecek*

My hopes for the future are quite simple, but grand: May the entire world be so converted by the Gospel of Jesus Christ that there is a radical conversion to *love*, such that heaven dwells on earth. This is my greatest hope for myself, my children, and my grandchildren. It all begins with each one of us. We must so radically become disciples of Jesus Christ that our own lives convict others of the need for conversion *today*. We must become *love* personified.

—*Peggy Rowe-Linn*

Today's world can look so bleak. Hope is elusive, but I see so many amazing teachers and programs available to us, like Dynamic Catholic, that are exciting. Also, as a Catholic, I hope in the intercession of Our Lady.
—*Cathy Ludwick*

Today we had our fourth child baptized, and as I stood there listening to the promises of the Catholic Church, I smiled, knowing we have it all right here. God is so amazing and so gracious to us. As we ended Mass today, the whole church was filled with the cries of many little children, for Mass took a little longer than expected for those who didn't know there was a baptism today! My husband and I smiled at one another, and I said, "This is the future of the Church, and man, is it loud!" I pray that volume and enthusiasm continues so our children and grandchildren and generations beyond truly have a place to call home, that they may understand why it is they practice the faith and that they truly embrace it with all the joy and boldness and faith of a child. May our Church truly be reignited and set on fire!
—*Melissa Winner*

My hope for the future of the Church is that *all* Catholics will believe in the true presence of Christ in the Eucharist.
—*Kathy Komaromy*

I hope we will all make God number one in our lives. I hope that there will be increased attendance at Mass and other religious services, as well as improved respect. I hope we will understand the importance of little things such as genuflecting in front of the

altar, being on time, and not leaving early at Mass, and appreciating the beauty and importance of the sacraments, especially the Eucharist.
—*Mary Knesis*

As a Catholic, my hopes for the future are that we, the human race, come to know and understand that we are one family sharing our common home, Earth. That our hearts are filled with so much love that we are compelled to care for each and every member of our family and joyfully tend to our shared home. For the time we are here, we should be in a dress rehearsal for heaven!
—*Marcia McMillen*

I have so much hope for the future as a Catholic. I feel we can save the world.
—*Marie Norton*

I feel hopeful as I see young families celebrating our faith in so many ways. Recently a young couple I know incorporated an hour of Adoration as a part of their marriage rehearsal evening! That's HOPE!
—*Barbara Botti*

My hope for the future is that the Holy Spirit may rekindle the hearts and minds of so many Catholics who don't have a relationship with Jesus. It's NEVER too late.
—*Nick Riebsomer*

As a Catholic my hopes for the future are that Mary's Immacu-

late Heart will triumph and that we will have a new spring in our Church with a boom of vocations and holy families!
—*Name Withheld*

I hope that people can see the joy of the Church, and the Church can experience a "rebranding" as a welcoming, loving home.
—*Sarah Thomas*

As a Catholic, my hope for the future is that we continue to engage the younger generation. I love to see young families at Mass, and especially engaged fathers, stepping up to be the head of the family in faith. It all begins with the family.
—*Pauline Teahan*

My hope for the future is that we will answer the call of the Catholic Church to bring about social justice in the world. I hope that we can be the leading voice against human trafficking and end slavery. By responding to this atrocity with rescue missions all around the world for those enslaved, ministries that prevent the vulnerable from falling into the trap of predators, and working to convert the hearts of traffickers, Catholics can heal a great deal of hurt and eradicate a lot of evil from this world. Imagine the image transformation of the Church that still struggles to recover from scandals of the past by being the answer to so many prayers for freedom and being a safe place.
—*Megan Proctor*

My hope for the future is a Catholic Church that is vibrant, inviting, energized, and standing for truth, justice, and goodness. I want the Church to be a beacon of hope and light in the world.

That we be peacemakers and lovers of all people is my dearest hope. Being a conduit of God's love is our mission.

—*Carole Ambroziak*

As I look forward to the future of the Catholic Church, I am so energized by the youth. I believe the Catholic faith in our young people is growing stronger than it has been in the past few decades. The images and stories from World Youth Day are inspiring. The strong examples in my own parish who are involved in youth groups, serving at Mass, and going on retreat bring me great hope. I pray that their active presence and energy bubble over to others and that they will instill their love of God and the faith in the generations to come.

—*Lesley O'Rourke*

My hope for the future is that the Catholic Church can stand tall and make just enough and the right kind of noise to have everyone take notice and want to find out what we're doing to make such a positive impact on our world. I think Pope Francis is working hard to that end, showing what unconditional love, peace, and human sanctity is. Hopefully people will stop and listen to see how easy it really is to live in a world of peace and harmony, really caring that they make a difference. The only way to do this is to embrace Christ!

—*Molly Morgan*

I was impressed by St. John Paul II's encyclical "Toward the Third Millennium," where he talked about a "new springtime" in Christianity. I thought at the time, *What on earth is he thinking?* It looked to me at that time (about when the sexual abuse scandal hit so many dioceses) that things were bad and would probably get worse. Still, after considering what the pope wrote, I began to recall some of the astounding prophecies found in Scripture— Jonah, the prophecies to David, the words of Jesus to Peter, and Paul's telling the Romans "where sin abounds, grace abounds the more." In light of these Scriptures, I began to think differently. If the Ninevites could convert so quickly, why couldn't our "culture of death"? If Paul is a reliable witness to what God can do, we should be in a tidal wave, a tsunami of grace that can move minds and hearts with unstoppable power. I believe that we will see mountains moved in this millennium, if not in our lifetime, if we are docile to the Holy Spirit.

—*Fred Schuhmann*

As a Catholic, I hope for a world with more saints, where more ordinary people are living lives that reach for holiness. I pray that every person will know how loved they are and, more importantly, will accept it in their hearts. The love of God can transform our lives and bring us to a self-awareness that sets us free. This freedom will help us to become the-best-version-of-ourselves.

—*Laura Becerra*

I hope for a Church, starting with my parish, that becomes well educated in the faith and strives to learn more—and experience more in prayer. I want my parishioners to understand that God is powerful and has a plan for every one of their lives and wants to intercede on their behalf if they let him. Given this strength of knowledge and experience, I also want it to permeate the lives of their friends and family and coworkers. I want them to love

going to Mass. And although times are tough and we have many challenges in our present-day Church, I want the Church to hold on to the hope that something amazing is about to happen.
—*Fr. David Aufiero*

As a Catholic, my hope for the future is that young Catholic parents will be courageous in their encouragement of the faith in their children. Our society tells us our children need to be involved in multiple activities, but as our young families stay busy, God gets crowded out. Young Catholic parents can stand up and take a different approach. Children should be given time to play, and dream, and sleep. Families must take time to bond, and work together, and learn about their Catholic faith together. Fathers especially need to find their voice as one of the family's spiritual leaders. Too often spiritual guidance is left completely to mothers. Children can sense if one parent has a lackluster attitude, and they will gravitate toward the easy way out. United parenting, with God as the family's single audience, will light a fire in the next generation of Catholics.
—*Karen DeCoster*

As a Catholic, what are your hopes for the future?

- That I will be a good Catholic for the rest of my life. (Jonah, age fourteen)
- That I'll continue to grow in my relationship with God. (Henry, age twelve)
- That my children will someday be Catholic. (Greta, age nine)
- Continue practicing my Catholic faith without judgment from others. (Agnes, age fourteen)

- That our children will continue to be practicing Catholics, and that any grandchildren will be raised in the faith. (Autumn, wife and mother)
- That the world will return to the predominant focus on the love of God and love for others over a love of self, and the Catholic Church in this country and around the world will continue to be a beacon of that selfless love. (Jess, husband and father)

—*The Sweley family*

As a young, active Catholic, I hope that the youth find the beauty in the Church. I feel people my age (eighteen to twenty-two years old) are turned away because they think that the tradition is too old, and they don't give the Mass a chance. I hope that young adults find meaning in the Mass, and I hope that the priests and Church leaders of this age can find modern ways to make the young people realize the genius of Catholicism.
—*Kayla Kroger*

I hope to grow every day into the-best-version-of-myself and the person who God is calling me to be. I hope to raise children that know the person of Jesus and always feel at home in the Catholic Church. I hope that the Church grows and flourishes in my lifetime to become the impetus for positive change in the world.
—*Katie Ferrara*

Star Lights For Starry I

A bedtime storybook
for children with Bible verses

by
Anne Mulcahy

First Edition,
First Printing 2005
©2003 by Anne Mulcahy
All rights reserved.

Published by
Anne Mulcahy
St. Louis, MO
annemulcahy2005@yahoo.com

Design by: J.Ryan Stanley
Illustrations by: Dan Shinn

Bible verses taken from King James Version
Thomas Nelson Publishers
Copyright permission granted

ISBN
0-615-12865-3

This book is dedicated to the memory of my parents, James and Johanna Mulcahy

Also to my niece,
Shannon Marie Murphy
And her brother,
Michael James Sweeney

I acknowledge
the kindness
of my Aunt,
Margaret Healy

I acknowledge that all good gifts come from heaven. I thank God for giving me the desire and strength to write and finish this book.

Special thanks to Shannon Murphy, my niece, who inspired the "Starry I" segment of this book.

Starry I Nights

poems

night 1 *Stop For Nature* (Faith) 10

night 2 *Joey* (Blessings) 12

night 3 *Dancing with an Elephant* (Clothes) 14

night 4 *Suzy* (Fear of storms) 17

night 5 *The Lady and the Button* (Being Confused) 19

night 6 *Those Sad, Bad, Lonely Days* (Being Sad) 22

night 7 *One Winged Butterfly* (Death) 25

night 8 *Mad at My Dog* (Being Mad) 28

night 9 *Who Made You?* (Creation) 30

night 10 *The Missing Sneaker* (Being Lost) 33

night 11   *Hugeo* (Fear of the dark) 38

night 12   *Martha* (Sharing) 41

night 13   *Lenny Lion Smells the Roses* (Pride) 43

night 14   *Freddy Come Lately* (Praying) 46

night 15   *Wishie the Fish E* (Wishing) 49

night 16   *Margaret and the New Hat* (Liking Yourself) 52

night 17   *The Gardener & the Writer* (Different) 55

night 18   *Talking Heads* (Worry) 57

night 19   *Mr. Thunder N. Clouds, Jr.* (Bad Friends) 60

night 20   *The Star Musician* (Joy) 62

shorter stories

night 21 *Sterling* (Being Mixed-up) 68

night 22 *Noto* (Salvation) 72

night 23 *Johanna In Without Land* (Obeying) 76

night 24 *Frank E. Fox Story* (Guidance) 82

night 25 *The Laughing Candle* (Time) 86

night 26 *Soabn, the Small* (Confidence) 90

night 27 *Sabrina* (Beware of strangers) 94

night 28 *Michael and the Green Lion I* (Pride) 97

night 29 *Michael and the Green Lion II* (Losing) *101*

night 30 *Michael and the Green Lion III* (Winning) 104

night 31 *Praise (a poem)* 107

short stories

Star Lights For Starry I

poems

night 1
(Faith)

Dear Starry I,

When the summer's hot sun comes, do you like to swim in the blue ocean? And in the winter, do you like to feel the cold breeze on your face while playing outside in the snow?

I wrote this poem to show you that the things you see with your "starry" eyes were made by someone you cannot see.

Stop for Nature

How many times
Do you
Look up at the sky
To see the morning sun
The clouds by chance
The moon at second glance
While falling asleep
Counting the stars
All the way to Mars?

How many times
Do you
Stop and feel
The breath of fresh air
Always, always there?

How many times
Do you listen
For instance
To the lonely hawk
Cawing in the distance?

How many times
Do you
Thank God
For making everything
Yes, everything
From the color "blue"
To the cow that says, "Moo"
To you and me?

10

Oh Starry I,
Please read with me verse 16 from chapter 1 of the 1st
book in the Bible called Genesis:

> And God made two great lights;
> the greater light to rule the day,
> and the lesser light to rule the
> night: he made the stars also.

This Bible verse helps you to know that the sun, moon and the
stars that you can see with your natural eyes were made
by a God you cannot see with your eyes. Accepting the Bible
verse as the truth, is an act of faith.

I am so glad that God made you!

goodnight, Starry I

night 2
(Blessings)

Dear Starry 1,

What does the word "Blessings" mean to you? It may sound like a strange word but "blessings" can be defined as the things that make you happy. I know you have a long list of things that make you happy.

I wrote this poem about a clown who wanted to be a "blessing" to others by making them laugh.

Joey

Joey is a happy clown.
He travels with the circus from town to town.
Laughter is the only sound that is found when Joey is around.
He makes as many children smile, as there are stars in the sky.
He wears a smile that is so big.
And his hair looks like a mop not a wig.
And on his face is a huge red nose.
And out of his flapping black shoes flop his toes.
Whenever he trips on his toes, he stops.
But the hat on his head still hops.
And if you think that is funny,
when he lifts up his hat on his head sits a bunny.
Children laugh very quick, after each and every trick.

Oh Starry I,

Read with me verse 17 from chapter 22 of the 1st book in the Bible called Genesis:

That in blessing I will bless thee, and in multiplying, I will multiply thy seed as the stars of heaven and as the sand which is upon the sea shore; and thy seed shall possess the gate of his enemies;

God promised in this verse to bless a man named Abraham and all his children. You are Abraham's child when you accept Jesus as your personal Lord and Savior. And Jesus blesses you each day.

You are a blessing to me!

goodnight, Starry I

night 3
(Clothes)

Dear Starry 1,

I know that there are days that you are very concerned about the clothes that you wear to school or even around the house. And there are days that you just do not care how you look.

Sometimes, you can get stuck thinking too much about how you look rather than what you are doing.

I wrote this poem for you about two funny-looking characters that were more concerned about what they were doing than what they were wearing.

Dancing with an Elephant

Once I saw a horse
Dressed in a green pokey-dot
Three piece silk suit
with a blue cowboy hat
and four red suede shoes
Dancing with an elephant
Who was dressed in a size two

Pink pant suit
with a yellow leather cap
and four brown sneakers

They were dancing through a wheat field
And when the music stopped
I ran right up to the horse
And asked

14

"Do you think it is proper to mix and match?"
"Mix and match!"
laughed the horse
"Yes, Mix and match that
silk suit with a cowboy hat!"
said I.

Then, the horse looked me
Straight in my eyes
And answered
"If I were you,
Probably not.
And if I were the President of the United States
Then, definitely not
And if I were your best friend
Then, certainly not

And if I were the King of Egypt
Then, most likely not

But I am just me
A horse
Not a clothes horse
Just a horse
Therefore, what I wear
I do not really care
As long as I am enjoying
What I am doing
Which is dancing with my friend,
this elephant."

Then, the horse
Took off the cowboy hat and threw it away
And looked me straight in the eyes
And said
"Let's not fight
It makes a lot of horse sense to dress right
So, turn on the music and let's dance!"

Oh Starry I,
Read with me verse 1 from chapter 12 of the last book in the Bible called Revelation:

AND there appeared a great won-der in the heaven; a woman clothed with the sun, and the moon under her feet, and upon her head a crown of twelve stars:

Imagine a woman dressed with the sun, moon and stars? This verse shows you that God is aware of what you are wearing but he doesn't want you to get unhappy about clothes but rather enjoy what you are doing!

goodnight, Starry I

16

night 4 (Fear of storms)

Dear Starry I,

Do you lie in your bed shaking with fear when a storm comes with thunder and lightning? I wrote this poem for you on those stormy nights!

Suzy

The clouds grew black
It was almost night
And little baby sister was asleep
Under the covers tight

But big sister, Suzy was wide-awake
Scared as the lightning flashed
And the thunder clashed

Suzy shook, shuddered and shivered
As her lips turned blue
And her teeth rattled, too

"Oh dear," cried Suzy
"What shall I do?"

"I cannot scream for Mommy or Daddy
My throat is too dry
And my bed is too high
And I will wake my baby sister
Who will never stop crying,"
Suzy kept sighing.

"Oh, I know what I shall do,"
cried Suzy.
"I will pray to Jesus
The Bible says that He is the bright and morning star
He will take away my fear
I will keep praying until He sends His angel near
Right here
In my dark room
Jesus will send help very soon."

"Oh, come quickly, Lord Jesus
Wherever You Are
Because my Bible says that you are
the Bright and Morning Star!"

Oh Starry I,

Read with me verse 16 from chapter 22 of the last book in the Bible called Revelation:

I Jesus have sent mine angel to testify unto you these things in the churches. I am the root and offspring of David, and the bright and morning star.

Jesus will shine His gentle light on you and chase away the storm clouds of fear!

goodnight, Starry I

night 5 (Being Confused)

Dear Starry I,
I know that you can get upset when you are explaining something to your Mom or Dad and they don't know what you are talking about. And you can get upset when you don't understand something that you are learning in school.

I wrote this poem for you about a guard who was confused.

The lady and the button

Once a lady
With lots and lots of cash
In her pocketbook stashed
Decided on a sunny Saturday afternoon
To dash into her car and take a ride
Through the countryside

Painted on a door
Of an old antique store
In small country town
Was a sign hanging upside down
Reading," Lots and Lots of buttons for sale inside"

So, the lady parked her car in a lot
And ran through the door of the antique store
Only to find the buttons mixed up in a large pot

She thought it might be very wise
Not to gaze on every button with her eyes
So, she closed her eyes

And pulled out two buttons from the whole lot
If she didn't like the first one
Then, she might like the second one

The first button was a portrait
Of a lady dressed in blue lace
And the second button was a picture of none other
Than President McKinley's face

The next day, the lady
Wearing a blouse of pink lace and on her collar
The button with President McKinley's face
Went to visit the New York State Capital Building
In the city of Albany

A security guard checked each and every visitor
Who walked through the door
Of the Capital building's first floor

When the guard saw the woman
Dressed in a blouse of pink lace
He asked whose face was on the button of her collar

"McKinley." replied the lady
"What did you say? asked the guard
"McKinley." replied the lady

The guard looked puzzled
"Why do you have a picture of your kidney on your
collar?" he asked.

"McKinley, not my kidney!" sighed the lady.
Does McKinley sound like my kidney?" asked the lady.

"Yes." said the guard.

Oh Starry I,

Read with me the 9th verse of chapter 3 of the
Old Testament book called JOB:

Let the stars of the twilight thereof be
dark; let it look for light, but have none;
neither let it see the dawning of the day:

In this Bible verse, the man named Job is so confused about
what is happening in his life that he wishes that there was no
new day. Even you, as a child, can get upset and feel lonely
when you are confused.

Starry I, it isn't fun to be confused. But God knows all about
you. He will lovingly help you get through those
confusing times.

goodnight, Starry I

night 6
(Being Sad)

Dear Starry 1,

I know that there are days that you are, just not happy. And you really don't want anyone to try to cheer you up on those "sad" days.

Telling you that everyone has those "sad, bad, lonely days" doesn't seem to make you feel any better. I wrote this poem just for you about those "sad" days.

Those Sad, Bad, Lonely Days

When a sneaky bee
Flies down from an old apple tree
And stings you on your knee

OR

You slip and fall
Running down the stairs and through the hall
Scrapping you elbow on the wall

OR

A shaggy-faced dog with brown eyes so sad
Snatches a cookie meant for you
From the hand of your Dad
And makes you mad

OR

The bases are empty
You're up to bat
The score is one to zero
It is the championship game
The bottom of the ninth
And you hit the ball
Way, way out
Toward the outfield wall
And your eyes look up

As the ball flies so HIGH
Then, lands in the glove
Of the outfielder
Who is standing so tall
Now, you want to hide your face
As the umpire makes the call
"You're out!"
And instead of high fives
Your teammates' mouths drop
With resounding sighs
"Oh, no!"

Oh, those sad, bad, lonely days
When everything seems to go wrong
It is on those days
That you need to know
That Jesus has you on His mind
And He is always so kind
He will help you find
So, many different ways
To get through " those sad, bad, lonely days."

Oh Starry I,
Read with me verses 3
and 4 of Psalm 8:

When I consider thy heavens, the work of thy fingers, the moon and the stars, which thou hast ordained;
What is man, that thou art mindful of him? and the son of man, that thou visitest him?

This Bible verse tells you that although God is Great and made the universe, He still has time to think about you.

Doesn't that make you feel better knowing that God is actually thinking about you on your "sad" days?

goodnight, Starry I

night 7
(Death)

Dear Starry I,

I will never forget hearing about the time a girl came home from a school musical concert and found her pet hamster named "Miss Bloom" laying lifeless in her cage. She was not asleep. She was dead. Oh, how the girl cried.

It is hard to understand why pets die. And it is even harder to know why people die.

I wrote this poem for you about a butterfly that died.

One Winged Butterfly

Once a tiny, tiny egg on a leaf
But not always a tiny egg
As it turned into a "hairy cat"
Called a caterpillar

Not always a caterpillar
For it turned itself upside down
And hanged from a leaf
With a hard shell covering
And it remained quiet, silent for awhile
But it did not always stay hanging upside down

As it split open the shell
And out came a many-colored thing
Called a butterfly

Oh, how this butterfly wanted to fly
Way up high in the sky
Toward the sun to have some warm fun
But the butterfly flew only half way to the sun
Because instead of having four wings
This butterfly had only one!

With only one wing
This butterfly had very little power
To travel from flower to flower
So, the butterfly flew to a bed of green grass
In a field of yellow dandelions
Softly, the dandelions' tears
Washed away the butterfly's fears
As the butterfly died.

I do not lie
The butterfly did die
And sometimes I wonder why

I do not lie
The butterfly did die
And sometimes I wonder why

Oh, why did the butterfly
Have to die?

Oh, why
Oh, why

Did the butterfly
Have to die?

Oh Starry I,

Read with me verse 11 from chapter 8 of the last book in the Bible called Revelation:

> And the name of the star is called Wormwood: and the third part of the waters became wormwood; and many men died of the waters, because they were made bitter.

Death was not God's plan for mankind. Death came because the first man named Adam disobeyed God's command in the Garden of Eden. God sent His only begotten Son, Jesus Chirst, to earth to become a man in the flesh. Jesus died on the Cross so that death would not hurt you any more.

So, death doesn't mean the end. It is really the beginning of a forever life.

If you accept God's gift of salvation through His Son, Jesus, your forever life will be in Heaven.

goodnight, Starry I

night 8
(Being Mad)

Dear Starry I,

    Do you ever get so mad that you run into the bedroom slamming the door behind you? And when you come out of your room, do you tell everyone that you are going to stay mad forever?

    Well, here is a poem for you about being mad.

Mad at My Dog

I am mad at my dog
Not mad as a dog
And you won't think it is funny
When I tell you why
I am mad at my dog
You may even want to cry

My father built a porch
Outside our front door
And the porch was painted blue and brown
And to me
It was the best porch in town

Well, do you know what my dog did?
She gave the porch a frown
As if to say it wasn't good enough
for her Royal Highness's crown
And walked over to the neighbor's porch
Where there was a doormat the color green

And sat there like a queen
Oh, how I wanted to scream
"Dog,
How could you be so mean?"

But I did not want to look like a fiend
So, I walked away
And haven't seen my dog
No, not since that day!

28

Oh Starry I,

Read with me verses 5, 6, and 7 of chapter 9 of the Old Testament book called JOB:

Which removeth the mountains, and they know not; which overturneth them in his anger.

Which shaketh the earth out of her place, and the pillars thereof tremble.

Which commandeth the sun, and it riseth not; and sealeth up the stars.

This Bible verse shows you how powerful God's anger can be. You do not want God to be mad at you.

And God does not want your anger to hurt others. God can help you get rid of your anger. When you get mad, just pray to God for His help and wait and see what He does for you.

goodnight, Starry I

29

night 9
(Creation)

Who made you?

Once a small boy looked up at the clear blue sky and asked:

Hi, sky
Way up high
I like looking at you
When you are so blue
Please tell me
Who made you?

The sky was silent. The boy twirled around. He looked up and he looked down. Then, he turned to the clouds and asked:

Hi, clouds
You look so white
In the sunlight
Can you tell me
Who put you in my sight?

The clouds were silent. The boy twirled around. He looked up and he looked down. Then, he turned to a tree and asked:

Hi, tree
Can you whisper
Through your leaves
And tell me
Who made you so magnificently?

The tree was silent. The boy twirled around. He looked up and he looked down. Then, he turned to an eagle and asked:

Hi, eagle
Soaring so high in the sky
Do you know who gave you
Those wings to fly?

The eagle was silent. The boy twirled around. He looked up and he looked down. Then, he turned to a fish and asked:

Hi, fish
I have only one wish
Tell me who made you
So, that I can eat you from my dish?

The fish was silent. The boy twirled around. He looked up and he looked down. Then, he turned to the dog and asked:

Hi, dog
Drinking from a pail
Who made you from
Head to tail?

The dog barked. The boy stood tall. And he said:

God made us all!

Oh Starry I,

Read with me verse 35 from the 31st chapter of the book of Jeremiah in the Old Testament:

Thus saith the LORD, which giveth the sun for a light by day, and the ordinances of the moon and of the stars for a light by night, which divideth the sea when the waves roar; The LORD of hosts is his name:

This verse tells you that God is the Creator of all things that you see in nature. Enjoy all of God's creation and take care of it!

goodnight, Starry I

night 10 (Being Lost)

Dear Starry I,

I know that you get upset in the morning before you go to school if you have lost a sock, a shoe, or a book. And it is super scary if you get lost in the grocery store and your Mom or Dad cannot find you.

I wrote this poem for you about being lost.

The Missing Sneaker

I am Marty's missing sneaker
I just fell out of the car
When his father stopped
On their first day of vacation
At the Grand Canyon

Marty was not wearing me
When I fell out of the car
I was on the floor
Marty opened the door
And accidentally kicked me out

He watched me
Falling, tumbling, sliding and rolling
Down a narrow cliff

I am all-alone down here at the bottom
Of the Grand Canyon
Marty must be sad
That he has lost his right foot's sneaker

The left foot's sneaker
Must not have anything to do
Now, Marty will have to find
A new pair of sneakers
To wear

I hope that a squirrel will not come
And make a nuthouse out of me
I hope the rain will not come
And make me soggy

Oh, if only Marty would find me
And save me from the bottom of this dark
Grand Canyon!

Oh Starry I,

Read verse 20 of chapter 27 of a New Testament book called Acts:

> And when neither sun nor stars in many days appeared, and no small tempest lay on us, all hope that we should be saved was then taken away.

The apostle Paul was in a situation where he felt lost with no hope of being saved. However, Paul found out that God delighted in rescuing him.

Asking Jesus into your heart, as your personal Savior, keeps you from being spiritually lost.

goodnight, Starry I

Star
Lights
For
Starry I

shorter
stories

night 11
(Fear of the Dark)

Dear Starry I,

I know that there are times in the dark nights that you get fearful. The darkness can cause even grown-ups to be fearful.

I wrote this story for you about a giant who learned to enjoy the dark nights.

Hugeo

Somewhere beyond the brightest star on a cloud lived a boy giant named Hugeo.

Hugeo floated across the heavens with a happy smile on his face during the daytime. But as soon as the sun set like a coin slipping into a pocket, Hugeo froze with fear like an over-sized popsicle. He was scared because he could not see what was happening all around him.

Hugeo tried to hide his face in his cloud but those big giant brown eyes popped out through the bottom of the cloud and that made him more scared because he saw nothing but darkness below him.

One night, Hugeo heard a strange noise above his cloud. He could not see what it was because of the darkness. He was so scared that he jumped up and ended up hanging from the side of the cloud.

Hugeo didn't want to look down at the endless darkness beneath his feet, so he looked up and saw that the strange noise was none other than an eagle flying by. The noise he heard was the wind beneath the eagle's wings.

But Hugeo saw something else when he looked up in the night sky. He saw tens, even thousands, and maybe millions or perhaps trillions of bright sparkling lights called stars.

Hugeo looked at a star that seemed to have a lot of points. He called the star "Pointed Ears." Then, another star was so so tiny that he called it "Miss Lite Head."

Hugeo fell asleep guessing the names of the stars.

When Hugeo awoke, his cloud floated near the rising sun. Hugeo did somersaults and flips on his cloud all day long until the night came again and he started to guess the names of more stars.

The nighttime became friendly for Hugeo when he called each star by a name.

Oh Starry I,

Read with me verse 4 of Psalm 147 in the Old Testament:

He telleth the number of the stars;
he calleth them all by their names.

This Bible verse tells you that God knows exactly how many stars are in the sky. He calls each star by its own name.

If God calls each star by name, then how much must He know all about you in the dark night.

goodnight, Starry I

night 12 (Sharing)

Dear Starry I,

I know that you like to share with others by drawing a picture. I knew a girl who liked to draw pictures of castles with American flags on them. She spent hours drawing them.

Sharing is a good thing. Sharing makes you feel good inside. I wrote this story about a girl giant named Martha who dreamed big dreams of sharing.

Martha

Beyond the darkest night on a cloud lived a girl giant named Martha. Sailing across the heavens on her cloud, Martha dreamt of great and noble acts of honor and fun. Especially, since tonight she was going to be a 1000 years old.

'Oh, how I'd like to share my birthday with all the children of the earth.' thought Martha. 'But what can I do?'

When Martha was a baby giant, she heard a bedtime story about a cow that jumped over the moon. 'If I caught that cow and milked it and sent the milk down in my giant bonnet, I could give drinks to all the thirsty children of the earth.'

With one giant eye on the cows in the fields on earth and the other eye staring at the moon, Martha waited for a cow to jump over the moon. But it didn't happen.

'Cows can't jump over the moon!' laughed Martha.

Martha caught a falling star. She put it in her pocket to crunch into thousands of pieces. She wanted to send a stardust storm down to warm the cold children of earth. Martha forgot that she had a giant-size hole in her pocket. The fallen star fell out.

'I will take a giant-size chunk off the moon. If it is made of cheese, I'll feed any hungry children of earth with cheese balls on my birthday.' thought Martha.

One giant-size bite of the moon was enough for Martha to say ugh! "The moon isn't made of cheese!" laughed Martha. Finally, Martha came up with a Giantly great idea. She decided to make her cloud into a cloud plane and draw a picture with her plane going from star to star like a dot to dot picture.

Martha made a giant-sized "happy face". On her birthday, Martha shared a smile with all the children of the earth.

Oh Starry I,

Read with me verse 28 of chapter 2 from the Book of Revelation:

And I will give him the morning star.

This is a short verse and easy for you to memorize. The verse tells you God will give you great blessings when you love Him and stay His child!

God is the best teacher on sharing! He gave you, Jesus, as your Savior!

goodnight, Starry I

night 13 (Pride)

Dear Starry I,

I know that you do lots of things well. It is good to always do your best. But that doesn't mean that you should think you are better than others. When you think you are better than others, you have pride inside of you. Pride is not a good thing. I wrote this story for you about a lion named Lenny who found out how bad pride can be.

Lenny Lion Smells the Roses

Lenny Lion strolled slowly through the jungle as his piercing eyes looked at every corner of his kingdom.

"I am the bravest, kindest, greatest, and the best King of this vast domain!" bellowed Lenny, the Lion, as he stood tall on the top of an anthill. His runny nose was pointed high up in the air.

"What did you say?" asked Eddy Eagle as he flew by. "Vast....what did you say?"

"I said domain. Must I spell it for you. D-O-M-A-I-N. It means place. I am the king of the vast place," shouted Lenny.

"Well, why didn't you say that in the first place?" asked Eddy Eagle.

"Did I hear someone spelling?" asked Bret Bee as his brother, Brad flew off a rosebush and buzzed around Lenny's runny nose.

"Let's have a spelling bee." suggested Brad Bee.

43

"I have no time for a spelling bee! I am much too important. I am the King of this vast domain," bellowed Lenny as he walked off the anthill. He yawned with boredom at Brad Bee's suggestion for a spelling bee. When Lenny closed his big mouth, he accidentally trapped the two bee brothers inside.

Brad and Bret Bee darted from one side of Lenny's big mouth to the other hoping their actions would cause Lenny to open his mouth and let them go free before he swallowed them alive.

As the bees flew every which way in Lenny's mouth, the lion crossed his eyes and danced around in circles. His tail was wrapped around his back legs and his front legs twisted together. He fell face down into a rosebush. His mouth opened and the bees flew out to freedom.

"These roses smell great," said Lenny "I didn't know what I was missing with my nose so high up in the air. It is time for me to come down to earth and smell the roses."

"How about a spelling bee now?" asked Bret Bee.

"Well, maybe that is a good idea." smiled Lenny. "Who can spell roses?"

"I can." said Bret Bee. "It is R - O - W - I - S."

"Well, that is a very good guess. But that is not right. It is R-O-S-E-S." gently answered Lenny not wanting to hurt Bret's feelings.

After all, the King of the Jungle didn't want to think of himself as better than anyone else in his jungle.

Oh Starry I,
Read with me verse 4 from the Old Testament Book called Obadiah:

Though thou exalt thyself as the eagle, and though thou set thy nest among the stars, thence will I bring thee down, saith the LORD.

This Bible verse shows you that God doesn't want you to have pride or think you are better than others.

goodnight, Starry I

night 14 (Praying)

Dear Starry I,

Have you ever thought about praying to God for help with your homework or what T.V. shows to watch? Prayer is simple. It is asking God for help. I wrote this story for you about a boy who prayed for a softball game.

Freddy Come Lately

Freddy was sitting on his cloud number 9 when he realized that he was late for angelic choir practice. Freddy was always late. And for angel to be late is not always a good thing.

Freddy tucked his harp under his arm and rushed to choir practice.

"Freddy, why are you extra late today? What happened to you? Never mind, I don't want to know. I have a message from the Angel of Assignments that he wants to see you right away. Hurry up, you are already late for his appointment." said the Choir Director.

Freddy rushed out of choir practice and flew to the Angel Of Assignments' office.

"I am so sorry for being late." said Freddy.

"That is perfectly okay. The Master asked, especially, for you. He has a special assignment for you. A boy named Pete Lobo has been praying every night. He is asking God to help him do well in the championship softball game tonight.

The Master knows all things and Pete will be up to bat tonight at 7:30 P.M." smiled the Angel of Assignments.

"Why does the Master want me? I am always late for all my assignments?" asked Freddy.

"The Master knows everything. He knows that you will be just right for this assignment." laughed the Angel of Assignments.

Freddy left the Angel of Assignments' office and decided to leave early to get to Pete Lobo's championship game on time. He flew over Boston en route to Chicago and found himself tossed by a thunderstorm. This storm was going to make him late for the game.

Freddy flew near to the ballpark in Chicago at 7:31 P.M.
Freddy was already one minute late.

Pete Lobo was up to bat and already had two strikes. The bases were loaded and the score was 3 to zero in favor of the other team. Pete was so scared as the pitcher threw a fast ball at him.

Freddy geared up his wings flopping extra hard plunging behind Pete in the batter's box. Freddy's wings caused a strong gust of wind to blow extra hard on Pete's bat as he swung. Pete hit a grand slam homer out of the ball park. Pete's team won 4 to 3. Pete was named the Most Valuable Player.

Pete looked up to heaven as his teammates surrounded him and carried him on their shoulders.

"Thanks, God for answering my prayer." he smiled.

Freddy, the angel, may always be late but God is never late!

Oh Starry 1,

Read with me verse 9 of Chapter 37
from the first Book of the Bible called Genesis:

And he dreamed yet another dream,
and told it his brethren, and said,
Behold, I have dreamed a dream more;
and, behold, the sun and the moon and
the eleven stars made obeisance to me.

In this Bible verse, a young boy named Joseph dreamt that
even the stars bowed to him. Joseph as a young boy loved
God and his dreams came true.

Praying to God helps your dreams come true.

goodnight, Starry 1

night 15
(Wishing)

Dear Starry I,

Sometimes you can wish for things that are possible but not good for you. You may wish to have an elephant for a pet. It may be possible but not very practical.

I wrote this story about a starfish that wished to be up in the night sky.

Wishie the Fish E

There was something very fishy about Wishie the moment he was born in the Pacific Ocean. He kept telling all the other fish of the sea that he wanted to get up in the night sky with all the other stars.

"You are a starfish and you can't shine like a star," insisted the lobster.

"If you were a catfish would you want to chase mice. Or, if you were a swordfish would you want to duel?" asked crab.

"I am going to get up in the night sky!" cried Wishie.

So, he hailed down a taxicab and told the driver to take him where all the other stars were shining.

The cab driver smiled and dropped Wishie off in Hollywood.

"I can see you in one of those cartoons!" laughed the cab driver. "Wait, before you get out of this cab take my sunglasses and wear them. It will make a better impression on the Hollywood producers!"

So, Wishie walked into the studio with sunglasses.

"Well, what do we have here?" asked the producer.

"I am Wishie and I want so much to be with all the other stars!" answered the fish.

"Well, let me see. We can put you on a children's television show with 10 other stars. And we will call it 'Wishie the Fish E counting His Lucky Stars!'" said the producer. "You can help the children at home watching by counting the stars. 1 2 3 4 5 6 7 8 9 10 lucky stars!"

"I want to be a star in the night sky!" said Wishie.

"How about a television commercial for soap. We will put soap suds on you and call it "Wishie Washy!" suggested the producer.

Wishie ran out of the studio and hailed a taxi to take him back to the ocean.

Oh Starry I,

Read with me verse 12 of chapter 22 from the Old Testament Book of Job:

Is not God in the height of heaven? and behold the height of the stars, how high they are!

This verse tells us that while you are on earth, you cannot climb up as high as heaven or even the stars. You need to be practical about some of your wishes!

goodnight, Starry I

night 16 (Liking Yourself)

Dear Starry I,

I know sometimes that children can say unkind words to other children. Children can make fun of how short, how tall, how skinny or how fat other children are. And sometimes other children's unkind words can make you not like yourself.

I wrote this story for you about a girl named Margaret who learned to like herself even when other girls made fun of her.

Margaret and The New Hat

In a small town named Zooie lived a young girl named Margaret. Margaret was the tallest girl in her class. The other girls in the class made fun of her calling her "giraffe girl."

Margaret had a sad face on most of the time in school. One day, Margaret was surprised when the most beautiful girl in the class came up to talk to her.

"Hi, Margaret." said the beautiful girl.

"Hi." shyly answered Margaret.

"Margaret, I want you to be my helper." said the most beautiful girl.

"Helper?" asked Margaret. "Why should I be your helper?"

"Because you are the ugliest girl in the class and if you will be my helper

then I will pretend to be your friend." said the beautiful girl.

52

"I don't think so." quietly answered Margaret as she walked away from the girl.

That night, Margaret cried herself to sleep.

She had a dream. In the dream, a King lived in the town of Zooie. He sent a letter to Margaret on royal paper inviting her to his palace.

Margaret did not go. He sent another letter and another letter and another letter but Margaret still didn't go to the palace.

Finally, there was a knock on the door. Margaret opened the door and saw a young girl carrying a box wrapped in gold paper with a gold bow on it.

"Hi, my name is Kelli. I am a messenger for the King. Here is a gift from him." smiled the girl as she ran away.

Margaret read the card before opening the gift. It read:

"Margaret, every night I climbed the highest mountain and caught a falling star with my star catcher. I caught 365 stars. It took a year. Then, I shrunk the stars in my star-shrinking machine and had 365 twinkles. Five twinkles made one tiny star. So, 365 twinkles made 73 stars. Then, I weaved the stars into this hat and sprinkled them with stardust paint. A beautiful hat for a beautiful girl! Love, from your King."

Margaret looked at the hat. It was brilliant with color and sparkled brightly. In the dream, Margaret wore the hat to school. It was invisible to everyone but Margaret. Margaret felt so beautiful in the hat that she began to smile at everyone. And everyone wanted to be around this happy girl.

Margaret woke up from her dream. She went to her closet to pick out an outfit for school. On the shelf, sat a box wrapped in gold paper with a gold bow on it!

Oh Starry I,

Read with me verse 3 of Chapter 12 of the Old Testament book called Daniel:

And they that be wise shall shine as the brightness of the firmament: and they that turn many to righteouness as the stars for ever and ever.

This Bible verse tells you that God wants you to be wise in how you act toward other children. Living a life close to King Jesus, makes you shine bright like a star. And you can accept who you are even if other children make fun of you. God doesn't make anything that is ugly.

goodnight, Starry I

night 17
(Being Different)

Dear Starry I,
Do you ever wish that you could sing, as well as, your best friend? Being different than other children can help make you all see that you need each other.

The Gardener and the Writer

Once there was a lady gardener in the town of Plantsville who spent most of each and every day planting new flowers and watering old flowers. She had the most magnificent garden in all of Plantsville.

Once there was a lady writer in the city of Pencilville. She wrote stories about the people of Pencilville and the surrounding areas. She wrote the best stories in Pencilville.

One day, the lady writer traveled through Plantsville on her way to the village of Nextown. She stopped when she saw the most beautiful flower garden that her eyes had ever beheld.

"I have never seen so many flowers in my life," exclaimed the lady writer. "I must write a story of your very own glory."

"But you cannot write a story of my very own glory." answered the lady gardener.

"But why?" asked the lady writer.

"Because I can't read." cried the lady gardener. " And I am afraid to learn."

"Oh, how sad." said the lady writer. "I have an idea. I will teach you how to write your own story of your own garden. If you can learn to write, you can learn to read."

So, the lady writer came every day with a big dictionary to the garden of the lady gardener. The lady gardener looked up words like "starflowers" and "sunlight" until she wrote a very long story.

One day, the lady gardener picked up the newspaper. She read the story that she wrote about her garden on the front page.

Then, the lady gardener became the lady "gardener-writer" and the lady writer became the lady "writer-teacher."

Oh Starry I,

Read with me verse 41 of chapter 15 of the New Testament book called the 1st Corinthians.

There is one glory of the sun, and another glory of the moon, and another glory of the stars: for one star differeth from another star in glory.

This Bible verse tells you that each star is different from another. You are different from your best friend and that is okay. Your differences can help you learn your need for other people in your life.

goodnight, Starry I

night 18 (Worry)

Dear Starry I,

Do you know what the word "worry" means? It means that you are fretful about things that might happen. You can "worry" about a test in school or making the swim team. It is not good to worry.

I wrote this story about some heads of lettuce that worried too much. And what they worried about didn't happen.

Talking Heads

"Let us go to the market right now," yelled the farmer from the field of lettuce to his wife on the farmhouse porch.

"Sounds like a great idea. I'll be ready in five minutes!" answered his wife.

"Did you hear what the farmer said to his wife. 'Lettuce go to the market,'" cried Baby Lettuce.

"We have only five minutes left here," cried Crispy Lettuce.

"I am too young to go to the market," said Baby Lettuce.

"Wait. Wake up Crabby Lettuce and ask him what we can do to stop the farmer from taking us all to the market." said Leafy Lettuce.

"Wake up, Crabby Lettuce, we need your help!" cried Baby Lettuce. "The farmer is going to take us to the market, now."

"Where are the farm workers and the trucks if we are all going to the market?" asked Crabby Lettuce.

"Crabby Lettuce is right. We should keep our eyes open and see if the trucks are coming to take us all away." said Leafy Lettuce.

"Look, the farmer is getting into his car. We are safe." said Baby Lettuce.

"What did the farmer say anyway?" asked Crabby Lettuce.

"He said 'let us go to the market now'" said Crispy Lettuce.

"The words 'let us' and the word 'lettuce' are very different words!" laughed Crabby Lettuce. "Worry, when you heard the word "SALAD!"

Oh Starry I,
Read with me verse 22 of chapter 10 of the Old
Testament book called Deuteronomy:

Thy fathers went down into Egypt with threescore and ten persons; and the LORD thy God hath made thee as the stars of heaven for multitude.

This Bible verse tells you that God's chosen people, the Israelites, were worried at times that they would not increase as a people while being in the country of Egypt. No matter how small you are, Starry I, God will help you grow! So, don't worry!

goodnight, Starry I

night 19 (Bad Friends)

Dear Starry I,

I know that your Mom or your Dad are very careful about the friends that you make. They want you to grow up with good thoughts and desires. Having just one bad friend, can make your life unhappy.

I wrote this story about one bad friend.

Mr. Thunder N. Clouds, Jr.

Mr. Thunder N. Clouds, Jr. was a boy giant who lived on not one cloud but three or four clouds at one time. Mr. Thunder N. Clouds, Jr. put his entire giant clothes into giant cardboard boxes and his giant shoes in giant paper bags and spread them out on three or four clouds while he traveled throughout the sky.

One day, he decided that he wanted to become the sun's friend. So, he parked his four clouds near the sun. He enjoyed living near the sun during the winter months.

But the giant thought that the sun was too hot to live near during the summer. So, he had an idea. He reached down to the ocean and threw giant handfuls of water on the sun. The sun was burning mad and kicked Mr. Thunder N. Clouds, Jr. out of the day. Then, Mr. Thunder N. Clouds, Jr. lived in the night. He liked the dark. Until, one night all the stars popped out near his clouds and kept him awake.

Mr. Thunder N. Clouds, Jr. made a lot of noise all over the sky looking for the Main Star Switch to shut off all the stars. But he couldn't find it. So, he had an idea. He took his giant hand and grab some mud from the earth and threw it on all the stars to make them stop shining.

The stars were surprised at getting mud thrown in their faces. So, they kicked Mr. Thunder N. Clouds, Jr. out of the night.

Presently, Mr. Thunder N. Clouds, Jr. is living in the dawn.

Oh Starry I,
Read with me verse 20 of chapter 5 of the Old Testament book called Judges:

They fought from heaven; the stars in their courses fought against Sis'-e-ra.

Sisera was an enemy of God's people and even the stars turned against this bad person.

goodnight, Starry I

night 20
(Joy)

Dear Starry I,

Joy is a feeling that is hard to explain. It is "happiness" inside of you that makes you smile. Joy is like a "pink cloud" that surrounds you while you are in a room inside your house.

The Star Musician

One night, a star named Astra had an idea. She thought that it would be good for all the stars to sing a gentle song at night to wish every child on earth peaceful dreams while sleeping. So, Astra wrote the words and music to a night song. She handed out the sheet music to every star that was shining that night.

The stars enjoyed singing together. They almost sounded like the angels. The words of the song were:

"Sleep, sleep
Dream, dream little children
Rest those "starry eyes"

Then, Astra thought that the morning stars needed to learn a wake up song for all the children of the earth. She wanted every child to wake up with a shout of joy.

So, Astra wrote a morning song. The words were:

"Wake up, wake up
Little children
From your sleep of night
Open those starry eyes
To a new day's light
Shout for joy
Both girl and boy."

The children shouted for joy when they woke up!
And Astra was named the Star Musician by all the stars!

Oh Starry I,
Read with me verse 7 of chapter 38 from the
Old Testament book called Job:

When the morning stars sang together,
and all the sons of God shouted for joy?

If God can make the stars sing together, then He can make
you wake up happy in the morning.

goodnight, Starry I

short stories

night 21 (being mixed-up)

Dear Starry I,

When your Mom pushes you on a swing, do you ever think that if you swing too high that a big cloud will come down and pick you up?

Thinking that clouds can come down while you are on a swing is being mixed-up or unclear about how things really are. I wrote this story for you about a mixed-up skunk.

Sterling

Sally S. Skunk looked fondly at her youngest baby born only three weeks ago. The other three baby skunks born at the same time seemed to be growing faster and had already opened their eyes.

"Stay here, Sterling. Your three baby brothers are already on solid food. So, I'm going to hunt for mice, insects and fallen fruit for them. I'll be right back to give you some milk." gently spoke Sally as she ran quickly to a nearby field. Her four youngsters were born in the countryside near the Hudson River in New York State.

Sally and her skunk family only lived one hour from New York City. Sally wished that the city that was nicknamed "The Big Apple" really was an apple so that she could feed her family on it for the rest of their lives.

Sally hurried her hunt for food because she wanted to get back to baby Sterling before dark. She worried about Sterling because he was still blind. After three weeks, baby skunks usually received their sight but not Sterling. He was still small, bald and blind.

"Mama!" cried Sterling from his place in the field. He missed his Mama and wanted to find her. Sterling crawled and rolled through the field to the nearby highway.

Sterling heard noises but did not see all the cars and trucks on the road. Horns were beeping at him as he crawled over the highway and rolled into a nearby truck stop. He crawled into something warm. Sterling didn't know that he crawled into a crate that a truck driver took out of the truck to sit on as he rested at the truck stop. Sterling only knew that he was warm and so comfortable in the crate.

"I better get this shipment to Saks Fifth Avenue. It is the stuff that makes women smell like skunks!" laughed the truck driver as he loaded the crate with Sterling in it onto the truck.

"Oh, lucky you." said the other truck driver. "I just have a load of bologna to deliver in my truck."

'Oh, my' thought Sterling. 'The man said he has a truck load of something that smells just like me.' An hour later, the truck arrived a Saks Fifth Avenue at the shipping and receiving department.

A woman in a pink suit ran up to the driver. "Is that the perfume shipment?" asked the lady. "Yes, madam." smiled the truck driver.

"Can you take one crate to the perfume department right away? asked the lady. "We are completely out of perfume."

"Sure." answered the truck driver as he grabbed the crate carrying Sterling, the baby skunk.

Sterling was so excited because he was going to the perfume department and the truck driver said that perfume smelt like skunks and Sterling was a skunk.

"Here ladies is your perfume. Hope it makes you smell like a skunk." laughed the driver as he left the crate with Sterling and the perfume on the counter. The sales lady was so happy as she started to unload the crate of perfume bottles. Sterling jumped up from the crate and stood on the counter. The sales lady fainted when she saw Sterling.

A woman with an umbrella came to the perfume department. When she saw Sterling, she screamed and tried to hit him with the umbrella.

Sterling did the natural thing for a skunk. He lifted his tail and fired an oily yellow liquid from his two highly specialized anal glands. Now, the woman customer was sprayed with a new fragrance called "Sterling".

"Oh, no. Oh, no." screamed the lady. "I smell like a skunk!"

Sterling was so confused. He thought perfume and skunks smelt the same and that women wanted to smell like skunks. Women were running and screaming, "Skunk!" Sterling jumped off the counter and ran out of the store. He ran as fast as he could until he found the field where his mother and brothers lived. Sterling's mother was so happy when she saw him.

"Oh, Mama, I was in the perfume department at Saks Fifth Avenue. I sprayed a woman with my scent and she screamed." cried Sterling.

"Oh, Sterling. You can see now. I am so glad." smiled Sally Skunk. "The scent of perfume and the scent of a skunk are not alike."

"Well, I am glad that I am home now with all the other skunks." cried Sterling.

Oh Starry 1,
Read with me verse 7 of chapter 32 of the Old
Testament book called Ezekiel:

> And when I shall put thee out, I will cover the heaven, and make the stars thereof dark; I will cover the sun with a cloud, and the moon shall not give her light.

Imagine the sun, moon, and stars not giving light.
Being in the dark would make it hard for you to live.
Being mixed-up can make you feel like you are walking
in the dark. God doesn't want you to be mixed-up.

When you feel mixed-up, you can pray to Jesus
and he will help you.

goodnight, Starry 1

night 22 (Salvation)

Dear Starry I,

Do you know what salvation means? It is Jesus saving us from all the sins and wrong things in our lives. Without Jesus, you really don't know how to live right. I wrote this story for you about a boy named Noto who found out how much He needed to be saved.

Noto

The land of children was a happy place. Everyone in the land of children was happy. Did I say that everyone in the land of children was happy? Not so. Only the children who asked the King into their houses were happy. There was one unhappy child in the land. His name is NOTO. Say "no" "to" everything and you will end up with a name that is "NOTO."

Noto sat on a table and ate his cereal from a chair. He used a fork instead of a spoon and the milk dripped down his T-shirt that was on inside out.

Finally, the day came when Noto was tired of being alone. He went for a walk in the land. First, he walked by Kristen's house. He heard laughter and music coming from Kristen's house. Kristen poked her head out the window and saw Noto.

"Noto, come to my party! When I asked the King into my house, he gave me the gift of friendship." smiled Kristen.

Noto didn't answer Kristen. He kept walking. At the park he met a boy named Shane. Shane was putting a sailboat into the pond.

"Hi, Noto. Come play with my sailboat. Since I asked the King into my house, he gave me the gift of crafts. So, I made this sailboat." Noto ran home. He had an idea. He would make a gift for the King and travel to the palace. He'd ask the King to come into his house and give him the gift of laughter.

Noto looked in his toy box. Most of his toys were broken. He found the engine of a fire truck and the head of a bear. Noto glued the Teddy bear's head to the front of the fire engine and smiled.

"There!" laughed Noto, "Now, I have a gift fit for a King!"

Noto walked out of his house and looked for road signs showing the directions to the King's palace. There were lots and lots of signs to the palace.

Noto walked on a very narrow road until he came to a sign that said the "The King's Highway." As the dark night came, Noto had to climb a steep mountain on the King's Highway. Suddenly, there appeared a bright star in the sky. Noto kept one eye on the star and the other eye on the gift that he made for the King.

Noto pushed and pulled himself to the top of the mountain. At the mountain peak, Noto looked down and saw the star shining above the palace. He was so excited that he accidentally let go of the toy. The fire engine with the teddy bear's face bounced and slide down the mountain at a very fast speed.

Noto ran after the toy and finally found it as it fell into a water fountain in front of the palace.

"Oh no. My gift is soaked. And the Teddy bear's head is soggy." cried Noto. "But I came this far and I must ask the King to come to my house and show me the right way to do things."

Noto grabbed his soggy gift and ran up to the palace door. The servants were laughing as they all stared at Noto and his funny-looking gift.

"I came to see the King and I have brought a gift for him." said Noto.

One of the servants showed Noto to the throne room. Noto walked into the room only to see a very steep stairway leading up to the King.

"Noto, I am so glad to see you. I have been waiting a very long time for your visit." said the King. "What is it that you want?"

"Well, first of all I want to give you a gift." smiled Noto as he climbed the stairs to the King. "And then I want to invite you into my house. I am very sad. I want to laugh."

" I will come to your house now." smiled the King as he stood up and walked down the stairs to meet Noto.

The King hugged Noto and asked the name of the gift.

"It's a. It's a. It's a. It is a teddy truck!" smiled Noto.

Oh Starry 1,

Read with me verse 10 of chapter 2 of the Gospel of Matthew:

When they saw the star, they rejoiced with exceeding great joy.

This Bible verse tells you that those who were seeking to find the baby Jesus in Bethlehem were given the help of a shining star to guide them.

When you ask Jesus into your heart, He gives you the gift of Salvation.

goodnight, Starry 1

night 23 (Obeying)

Dear Starry I,

I know in school that sometimes you find it hard to sit at your desk and listen to your teacher. And sometimes you find it hard to listen to your Mom or Dad.

I wrote this story for you about a girl who found it hard to obey.

Johanna in Without Land

Johanna sat in her Math class looking out the window. Leaves were falling down from the branches of the trees. It was autumn. Johanna watched as one leaf floated and floated through the air and headed toward the open window near where Miss Numbers, the Math teacher, was standing.

"100 multiplied by zero is what, Johanna?" asked Miss Numbers as she turned from the blackboard and looked at Johanna.

"LOOK OUT, MISS NUMBERS! A HUGE LEAF IS HEADING TOWARD YOU FROM THE OPEN WINDOW!" screamed Johanna.

Miss Numbers threw her book in the air and hid behind her desk. Slowly, she lifted her head and saw the tiniest leaf sitting on the window sill. All the children in the class laughed as Miss Numbers turned red with embarrassment.

"Johanna, you will take a note home to your parents, tonight!"shouted Miss Numbers.

Johanna took the note and put it in her backpack. When she arrived home, she ran upstairs immediately in order to avoid seeing her mother. She turned on her radio loud so that she could not hear her mother calling her to come and set the dinner table.

Johanna ignored her mother's call to set the table and kept listening to the radio. As Johanna listened to the radio, she heard a tapping on her window and a little bird without wings called her name.

"What is a bird without wings doing at my window?" asked Johanna.

"I came to take you to Without land." said the bird. "Go to your closet and you'll find a door there."

As she opened the door to Without Land, she saw a sign that said "UNWELCOMED TO WITHOUT LAND." Johanna entered Without Land with the bird hopping along side her. Johanna noticed the trees were without leaves. The birds were without wings. The river was without water.

"This sure is Without Land." laughed Johanna. "The trees are without leaves. The river is without water and you are without your wings."

"You can call me "Hopalong" since that is what I do without my wings." said the bird. Johanna sat down under an old haggard apple tree without branches near a river without water.

"I wish someone would tell me what I am doing here. I do not like this place." cried Johanna. Hopalong sat near Johanna.

"I came here 10 years ago for not obeying the guide bird in charge of flights south in the winter. I kept stopping in cornfields and playgrounds. I was warned to stay with the flock but I didn't listen. Finally, the birds sent me to Without Land. My wings fell off when I arrived here." said Hopalong.

"And why are you here, river?" asked Johanna. "Did you open your big mouth too much?"

"Yes, that is why I am here." shouted the river. "I was the most talkative river on earth. I kept opening my mouth so much that I caused too many floods."

"Aren't you going to ask me why I am here?" asked the old apple tree. "I didn't like people. When families came near me to pick my apples, I just shook my branches and let the apples fall on their heads."

"I guess that I am here because I didn't pay attention in math class and I didn't listen to my Mom when she called me to set the dinner table." sighed Johanna. "I miss my Mom and Dad."

"I miss my wings!" said Hopalong

"I miss my water." said the river.

"I miss my apples and branches." said the old apple tree.

"There has to be some way to get out of this place!"exclaimed Johanna.

Then, Hopalong told a story that he heard. A Great Gentle Lamb lived on the top of the Golden Stairs. The lamb had the power to release things and people from Without Land. The only road to the Golden Stairs was the Golden Path.

"I know where you can get on the Golden Path. When you arrive at the top of the Golden Stairs, it is important that you tell the Lamb that you are truly sorry for why you came to Without Land." said Hopalong.

"That sounds so easy. Why hasn't anyone or anything tried to go to the Lamb sooner than this?" asked Johanna.

"Because of Wild Wolf. He is evil and he can change his appearance to look like anything. If he can get you off of the Golden Path just once, then you are doomed to be in Without Land forever. You can never get out of here. None of us wanted to risk being here forever." said Hopalong.

"Well, I am going to see the Great Lamb and ask him to forgive all of us." said Johanna.

River and old apple tree wished Johanna a safe journey. Then, Hopalong hopped with Johanna to the Golden Path.

"I wish you a good trip." smiled Hopalong. "Remember, Wild Wolf can disguise himself to be anything to get you off the Golden Path. But he can only try to fool you three times. So watch!"

"Thanks, Hopalong. I will see you soon," said Johanna.

Johanna turned away from Hopalong and slowly started walking down the Golden Path. Then, as it became dark, Johanna started to run faster and faster. As she ran, she saw a moving object in front of her. It was a flashlight.

'Oh, that flashlight would help me to see better.' thought Johanna.

As Johanna went to grab the flashlight, it moved off the Golden Path. Johanna would have to leave the path to get it. Then, she realized that it probably wasn't a flashlight but Wild Wolf disguised.

"You are not a flashlight. I know you are Wild Wolf." cried Johanna.

Suddenly, the flashlight changed into Wild Wolf.
"I still have two chances left to fool you." cried Wild Wolf.

Although Johanna was tired, she kept running down the path. But she was getting thirsty. She saw a water fountain near the path. She ran to get some water but the fountain seemed to move.

Johanna laughed and ran away from the fountain.

"I know that you are not a water fountain but Wild Wolf. You have only one more chance." laughed Johanna.

"The next disguise will be the best. I promise you!" said Wild Wolf.

As Johanna kept running down the path, she saw a bright light. She wondered if she was getting close to the Golden Stairs. Johanna saw a sign near the bright light. It gave directions to the Golden Stairs. Johanna leaned over the Golden Path to read the directions but the print was very small on the sign and she had a hard time seeing it. She leaned closer and closer to the sign and was about to fall off the Golden Path when she remembered that Wild Wolf had one more disguise.

"You are not a sign. You are Wild Wolf! I am free now," exclaimed Johanna as she jumped up and down. Johanna, suddenly, hit her foot on a rock and looked down to see that it was the first step of the stairs.

"The Golden Stairs!" shouted Johanna. When Johanna reached the top of the Golden Stairs, she saw a beautiful lamb sitting on a throne.

"Oh, Lamb please forgive me for not listening to my math teacher and also for not obeying my Mom." said Johanna.

"You are free, Johanna. Go home." smiled the Lamb.

"Before I go can you forgive Hopalong, river and the old apple tree and give them back their wings, water and branches?' asked Johanna.

"Yes. It is good that you care about nature!" smile the Lamb.

Oh Starry I,

Read with me verse 62 of the 28th chapter of an old Testament book called Deuteronomy:

And ye shall be left few in number, whereas ye were as the stars of heaven for multitude; because thou wouldest not obey the voice of the LORD thy God.

This Bible verse tells you that God's chosen people would suffer for not obeying Him. God wants you to obey your parents and respect your teachers.

goodnight, Starry I

night 24
(Guidance)

Dear Starry I,

Maybe, you would like to decide for yourself about what you will do everyday. But even grown-ups like your Mom or Dad need to ask other people for help or advice.

It is always good to let others teach and guide you in your young life.

I wrote this story for you about a newspaper reporter who needed the help of others to get the story he was writing.

Frank E. Fox Story

The editor of the Daily Nosey Newsy paper sent the "Fox" on his first writing assignment as a newspaper reporter. The editor's name was Fidget Gadget III.

"Now, listen to me, Fox. This is your first assignment as our new sports reporter. I have been told that there is going to be a race tomorrow and I need you to find out about it." said the editor.

"What kind of a race, boss?" asked Fox.

"I heard that it was a baby race." smiled the editor.

"But I am a sports writer. Why doesn't the children's editor cover this story?" asked Fox.

"Babies racing is still a sports event, my boy." smiled the editor.

"Well, I guess you are right." agreed Fox. "Say no more, boss. I am on my way."

Frank E. Fox walked out of the newsroom and onto the streets. The race was supposed to be somewhere in the vicinity of Kane and Main Streets. Frank saw a young boy digging for worms in his backyard.

"Hi, have you heard anything about a race with babies taking place around here tomorrow?" Frank yelled at the boy.

"Please, shhh. Do not talk about the race in front of my worms," cried the boy. Frank turned from the boy and saw a lady walking down the street with a bag of groceries.

"Hi, madam. My name is Frank E. Fox and I am the new sports writer for the Daily Nosey Newsy paper. Have you any idea about what kind of a race will be held here tomorrow?" asked the Fox.

"I know your editor Fidget Gadget III and if he told you that there is a race here tomorrow, then I am sure some little bird told him about it." said the lady.

Frank E. Fox was puzzled as to the kind of a race happening there tomorrow. Then, Frank saw a young girl swinging on a swing from a tree.

"Have you ever heard anything about a race, little girl?" asked Frank E. Fox.

"I only know that I am flying high enough right now to be in that race, myself," yelled the girl.

Frank E. Fox sat down near the sidewalk and looked over all his notes.

The boy said not to mention the race in front of his worms. The lady said that some little bird must have told the editor about the race. And the little girl said that she was flying high enough to be in that race.

"There are three clues and now I guess I should know what kind of a race it is." said Frank to himself.

Frank looked up in the sky and saw thousands of baby birds getting ready for the race.

The headline in the Daily Nosey Newspaper read "SOME BIRD BRAIN MAKES THIS YEAR'S FLIGHT SOUTH A RACING EVENT."

Oh Starry I,

Read with me verse 20 of the chapter 1 of the last book of the Bible called Revelation:

The mystery of the seven stars that thou sawest in my right hand, and the seven golden candlesticks. The seven stars are the angels of the seven churches: and the seven candlesticks which thou sawest are the seven churches.

In this Bible verse, you see that God has given seven angels to guide seven churches. God uses good people to help guide you to the truth in your young life.

God will guide you each day of life!

goodnight, Starry I

night 25 (Time)

Dear Starry I,

Have you ever wasted time while being bored? Time is a precious gift from God to us.

I wrote this story for you about a candle who didn't waste the time it was just sitting on a birthday cake before it was lit. This candle told jokes to the other candles. It wanted to be a stand-up comic!

The Laughing Candle

Max, the candle, always enjoyed his life on birthday cakes. Sometimes candles were put on the cake hours before they were lit and the child blew them out.

As Max stood on the cake, he made up jokes to tell the other candles.

Whether it was the fact that candles stood on cakes or birthday candles were for a festive event, Max down deep inside his waxiest self wanted to be a stand-up comic.

"Why did the chicken cross the street?" Max asked the other candles.

"Max, we have heard that one!" shouted the candles.

"No, this is a new joke on the chicken crossing the street," laughed Max.

"Okay, then why?" asked the candles.

"Because it just so happened that the chicken was standing in front of a fast food restaurant and it crossed the street so it wouldn't get fried." laughed Max.

"Oh." sighed the candles.

"Here is one that I was working on this morning. Two one dollar bills were walking down the street and one dollar says to the other dollar.

"Do you want to go to the store?" asked the dollar.

"Okay." answered the other dollar turning around to run home.

"Where are you going?" asked the one-dollar bill. "The store is not in that direction."

"I'm going home to change, I want to take the bus!" answered the other dollar.

The other candles roared with laughter. Max was happy.

"Here is another new joke. What vegetable never missed a day of school?" asked Max.

"What vegetable?" asked the candles.

"A turnip. It always turns up at school!" laughed Max.

As the birthday candles were lit, Max ended his comic act and became again just a candle on a cake.

Oh Starry I,

Read with me verse 2 of chapter 12 of an Old Testament book called Ecclesiastes:

While the sun, or the light, or the moon, or the stars, be not darkened, nor the clouds return after the rain:

This Bible verse tells you to seek God even when you are a child. Now is the right time to begin to read your Bible and learn about God.

goodnight, Starry I

night 26 (Confidence)

Dear Starry I,

I know that you sometimes do not feel sure about yourself. You can be shy or afraid that other children will reject you.

I wrote this story for you about a boy who learned to believe in himself.

Soabn, The Small

"Hurry up, Soabn. We are going down to Egypt!" called Soabn's cousin, Shannon. "My brother, David, is already in the caravan."

"I am coming!" answered Soabn. It was Soabn's first time away from Jerusalem. It was also his first time away from his mother and father. He was taking this journey with his Aunt Hannah and his two cousins, Shannon and David.

"I wonder if we will see some Egyptian pyramids or some mummies!" said Soabn as he reached his cousins in the caravan.

The journey was long and tiresome and at times the children had a hard time thinking of things to talk about.

"I know what we need to talk about" said Shannon. "Soabn, what does your name mean?"

"Well, I don't know. I never asked my mother or father."

answered Soabn. "I'll ask them when I go home."

"My name means 'the gift of God'," said David. "My mother and father named me in honor of King David of Israel."

"And my name means 'wise one'. "said Shannon." I just love the meaning of my name. And I think that you need to know the meaning of your name, Soabn!"

"Well, I don't think that I'll ever be a King of Israel, so what does it matter what my name means?" asked Soabn.

"It is good to know the meaning of your name. It gives us something to talk about until we get to Egypt," laughed Shannon.

The caravan stopped in a desert place. That night, the children were able to sleep outside under the stars. Soabn dreamt that he was living in Jerusalem in the time of the Kings. The people of Israel wanted to find a King and everyone started to say that Soabn would make a grcat King. Soabn was so surprised that the people wanted him as their King. But in the dream all the people started to ask the meaning of their King's name.

"Well, I don't know." answered Soabn. "I never asked my mother or father."

"Well, your cousin, David's name means 'the gift of God'. Your other cousin, Shannon's name means 'wise one'. So, your name must have a good meaning." said the people of Israel.

"Let's ask Shannon to figure out the meaning of your name." said the people of Israel.

"Well, since my name means 'wise one', I will take each letter of Soabn's name and find a word that begins with each letter. Give me a few minutes." smiled Shannon.

Shannon left to be alone to figure out the meaning of Soabn's name.

Soabn and the people waited in Jerusalem for Shannon to return with the meaning of Soabn's name. Crowds gathered in Jerusalem. The people wanted to make a parade for Soabn. They also made a gold crown to put on Soabn's head.

"King Soabn! King Soabn." chanted the crowds.

Soon, Shannon returned to the crowds. She had a frown on her face.

"I think I know what 'Soabn' means. I took the letters and found the word that matched the letter. His name means "Sort of a Big Nothing." See, how the first letter of those words spells Soabn." smiled Shannon.

"What!" laughed the people. "How can we have a King with a name that means sort of a big nothing?"

Soabn stood there with his mouth opened. Why would his mother or father give him a name that means "sort of a big nothing?"

"Shannon, how wise are you really? My parents wouldn't give me a name that means 'sort of a big nothing'" cried Soabn.

"Maybe, they wanted you to be humble!" laughed Shannon.

"Wake-up, Soabn. You are talking in your sleep." said David.

"Oh, David, I need to know the meaning of my name. I just had an bad dream about the meaning of my name." cried Soabn.

When Soabn arrived home from Egypt, he ran to his mother and asked the meaning of his name.

"'Star of a bright night' is the meaning of your name, Soabn!" smiled his mother. "The first letter in each word spells Soabn. A name fit for a King!"

Oh Starry I,

Read with me verse 2 of chapter 2 the New Testament Gospel called Matthew:

Saying, Where is he that is born King of the Jews ? for we have seen his star in the east, and have come to worship him.

This Bible verse tells you that people were seeking a king when a baby named Jesus was born in a manager in Bethlehem. Imagine a king born in a manager.

King Jesus is a loving Savior who treats you royally!

goodnight, Starry I

night 27 (Beware of Strangers)

Dear Starry I,

I know that you have been told by your Mom and Dad or your teachers in school to be careful when talking to strangers, especially, when you are all alone.

I wrote this story for you about a bad stranger.

Sabrina

As the toy maker painted the last black eyelash on the doll's face, he carefully set the doll on the front shelf of the store.

"Sabrina, someday you will make a lot of people happy." smiled the toy maker.

As the window shades were pulled and the store closed, Teddy D. Bear wasted no time in scolding Sabrina.

"Shame on you! So new and so beautiful and no one bought you on your first day in this store. Tomorrow, don't just sit there. Stand up and smile at everyone that comes into the store." said Teddy D. Bear.

The next day, Sabrina smiled and waved at all the store customers but nobody bought her.

That night, Carly, the Clown, cart wheeled over to Sabrina.

"Tomorrow make funny faces at the customers." suggested Carly, the Clown. "Then, someone will take notice of you."

The next day, Sabrina smiled, waved and made funny faces at the customers. But nobody bought her.

When the store closed that night, Peta Pony came up to Sabrina and said, "Sabrina leave this store and go out and search for a home. You will never find a home by staying here."

So, Sabrina ran out the door of the toy store before it closed and started walking down one street after another.

She met a toy robot transformer on one of the streets.

"Are you lost?" asked the strange toy.

"No." answered Sabrina.

"Can I help you?" asked the strange toy.

"No." answered Sabrina.

"Do you want some candy?" asked the strange toy.

"No." answered Sabrina.

"Can you help me find my missing cat?" asked the strange toy.

"No." said Sabrina as she ran away from the toy. She felt uneasy about that toy. The strange toy transformed into a snake and slide after her.

Sabrina yelled "Help, Help, Help."

She kept running. But the snake caught up with her. Sabrina kicked and screamed and even bite the strange toy.

Sabrina didn't know that the toy maker was searching for her. He walked down the same street that she and the strange toy were on. The toy maker grabbed Sabrina away from the strange toy.

"Be patient, Sabrina. It takes time to find the right home." smiled the toy maker as he carried her back to the toy store.

A few months later, a teacher came into the store and bought Sabrina. Sabrina enjoyed the rest of her life as a "classy" doll!

Sabrina smiled when the teacher taught the children to beware of strangers!

Oh Starry 1,

Read with me verse 13 of the book called Jude in the New Testament:

Raging waves of the sea, foaming out of their own shame; wandering stars, to whom is reserved the blackness of darkness for ever.

This verse shows you that some strangers may appear to be nice but they are not. Beware of strangers and stay close to your Mom or Dad.

goodnight, Starry 1

night 28 (Pride)

Dear Starry I,

What is pride? Pride is a sin that keeps you away from God. Pride is inside your heart and it makes you think that you are better than other people.

Pride can hurt other people's feelings. I wrote this three-part story for you. The first part tells you about a Green Lion who had too much pride.

Michael and the Green Lion Part 1

Michael lived in a park with lots of animals that were part of a zoo. There were games in the park for children to play. The park was a fun place to be. And Michael was named "the play keeper" by the park Master.

Michael always had lots of balloons and music for the children. The park Master gave Michael a special red sword. The sword was to protect the children and the animals from any danger. But Michael never once had to use the sword.

One day, Green Lion, the most beautiful and friendliest animal in the park wanted to speak to Michael alone. Michael was more than glad to speak to Green Lion. He truly admired and loved this amazingly beautiful creature.

"Michael, I want to be the play keeper of this park. I know I can do a better job than you." demanded Green Lion.

Michael was taken by surprise.

"The park Master made me the play keeper. I cannot give this job to you." answered Michael.

"I do not want to be just the most beautiful animal in this park." said Green Lion. "I want more. I want to be the most powerful animal in this park. And I want your red sword." Green Lion left Michael and returned to the Forest area of the park.

"Who wants me to be the play keeper of this park instead of Michael?" Green Lion asked the other animals in the forest.

One hundred animals shouted that they wanted to follow Green Lion.

"We must steal the red sword from Michael. Does anyone have any ideas on how to it? asked Green Lion.

"I can hide in a tree branch and make believe that I am stuck and call for Michael and you can come from behind and take the red sword" said baby Cub bear.

"I can run to Michael and tell him to hurry. He may forget to call Jesse, The Blue Lion, to be with him. Michael knows the park Master's rule is never to be alone for a rescue." suggested the cub bear's mother.

"That is a great idea. Let's do it." smiled Green Lion.

That afternoon baby cub bear hid in the tree branch and called for help. As planned, the cub's mother ran to Michael for help.

"Please, come. My cub is stuck in a tree branch," cried the mother bear. "Please hurry!"

Michael listened to mother bear's plea and broke the safety rule of the park. He went alone to a rescue.

Michael climbed the tree and bent down to untangle baby cub bear. Green Lion sneaked up behind Michael in the tree and grabbed the red sword from his side.

"You must be kidding, Green Lion. Why are you stealing my sword?" cried Michael as he turned from the baby cub.

"You cannot be the play keeper of this park without you red sword." said Green Lion. "I am going to leave this park now with my followers. I shall return in a few days to take over this park."

Michael stood at the entrance of the park. He watched Green Lion leave with his followers. Dark clouds began to form over the park.

....To be continued

99

Oh Starry I,
Read with me verse 13 of chapter 14 of the Old Testament book called Isaiah:

> For thou hast said in thine heart, I will ascend into heaven, I will exalt my throne above the stars of God: I will sit also upon the mount of the congregation, in the sides of the north.

This Bible verse tells you about someone who had pride in his heart. He wanted to be higher and better than God. No one is more powerful than God.

Reading the Bible and praying can keep pride out of your heart.

goodnight, Starry I

night 29 (Losing)

Dear Starry I,

In Part I of "Michael and the Green Lion," Michael made a mistake. He was not suppose to be alone during a rescue.

Even children make mistakes. I wrote part II of Michael and the Green Lion to show you that when you do make a mistake, you can turn to God for help.

Michael and the Green Lion Part II

"Michael, where is Green Lion? Also, why are there fewer animals in the forest." asked Jesse, the Blue Lion as he ran up to Michael at the park entrance.

"You missed it. Green Lion tricked me. He had mother bear call me to rescue baby cub from a tree limb. I went alone and that is when Green Lion sneaked up behind me and stole my red sword."answered Michael.

"Your red sword is stolen. You went on a rescue alone. You know the park Master's rule is never to be alone in a rescue. You broke the rule of the park." said Jesse.

"I know I made a big mistake. I have no way of protecting the children." sighed Michael. "And Green Lion promised to come back with the red sword and his followers to take over the park."

"You are going to have to go to the park Master and tell him what has happened. He will know how we can stop Green Lion from taking over the park." said Jesse, the Blue Lion.

"I am scared to go to the park Master. I am afraid to tell him that I made a big mistake." said Michael.

"Don't worry, Michael. The park Master is kind. He knows that we all make mistakes. You need him more than ever now. You don't have the red sword for protection." said Jesse.

"Climb on my back. I will take you to the Master." said Jesse.

Michael climb on Jesse's back and they began to ride through the Dark Woods to the Master's house. There were many strange sounds in the Dark Woods but Jesse told Michael not to listen. He believed that Green Lion was making those noises to scare Michael away from going to the park Master.

As Michael and Jesse came to the end of the Dark Woods, a flock of strange birds attacked them.

"Keep your head down." said Jesse. "I will run swifter than an eagle to get away from these birds. I know Green Lion sent them after us."

Jesse ran swiftly and reached the door of the park Master's house.

Michael knocked on the door and the Master opened it immediately.

"Oh, Master. I am so sorry to tell you that I made a big mistake. I did a rescue alone and Green Lion stole my red sword of protection. He wants to take over the park and be the play keeper." cried Michael.

The park Master forgave Michael and said, "You cannot allow Green Lion to take over the park. You will fight Green Lion with one word."

"A word?" asked Michael.

"Yes, when Green Lion comes use the word "zeebeemee." He will become powerless and he will drop the red sword and run out of the park." instructed the Master .

"But how can a word like "zeebeemee" stop a big strong lion with a red sword and his one hundred followers?" asked Michael.

"Just listen to me. And you will find out very soon how powerful one word can be." smiled the Master of the park. Michael and Jesse, the Blue Lion, left the park Master and returned to the park.

....To be continued

Oh Starry I,

Read with me verse 9 from Psalm 136 in the Old Testament:

> The moon and the stars to rule by night:
> for his mercy endureth for ever.

This Bible verse shows you that God is merciful. You can turn to Him when you fail or make a mistake. Always know that you can turn to God when you are right or when you are wrong.

goodnight, Starry I

night 30
(Winning)

Dear Starry I,

In Part III of Michael and the Green Lion, you find that Michael wins against the Green Lion by using the word "zeebeemee." As you grow in your faith, you learn to let God fight your battles.

Michael and the Green Lion Part III

Michael sat by the park gate where he once stood as the play keeper. He knew that Green Lion was going to return and try to take the park from him and the other children.

Michael would use the word "zeebeemee" when Green Lion returned with his followers to take over the park. Jesse, the Blue Lion, gathered all the children and hid them in the main pavilion.

As Michael sat by the park gate, he felt sad that there were no balloons, no music, and no laughter in the park since Green Lion stole the red sword. Michael wondered how a little word like "zeebeemee" could stop a powerful lion and his one hundred followers. But the Master knew all about his park, his red sword, and the Green Lion.

The wind howled. The clouds grew dark and finally Michael saw Green Lion coming over the mountain with his followers. They were marching in line like soldiers ready for a battle.

Michael hid in a tree branch over the entrance of the park. He planned to surprise Green Lion after he entered the park.

"Now, we will take over this park. We will not allow children to play here anymore!" laughed Green Lion as he entered the park.

Suddenly, Michael jumped off the branch and onto Green Lion's back. Green Lion shook off Michael and held the red sword high in the air.

"This is my park, now" laughed Green Lion.

Michael looked at Green Lion and in a quiet voice said, "Zeebeemee."

Green Lion looked scared. He dropped the red sword. He and all his followers ran out of the park.

Jesse, the Blue Lion and the children ran from the main pavilion and surrounded Michael.

Michael grabbed the red sword and cried "Victory!"

Oh Starry I,

Read with me verse 8 of the 5th chapter of an old
Testament book called Amos:

Seek him that maketh the seven stars and O - ri' - on, and turneth the shadow of death into the morning, and maketh the day dark with night: that calleth for the waters of the sea, and poureth them out upon the face of the earth: The LORD is his name:

There is no power greater than God's power. The power of
the Devil is not greater than God's power. Jesus' name is
powerful. In the name of Jesus, we have the Victory over
the Devil and all his evil forces!

goodnight, Starry I

night 31
(Praise)

Dear Starry 1,
It is time to say goodbye for now. When your Mom or Dad tells you how good you are, they are praising you. Here is a short poem for you about praising God.

Praise

Have you told God
Lately, how good He is
That is a way of praising Him
God does lots of little things
To bless you each day
And His biggest thing is sending
Jesus your way!

Oh Starry 1,
Read with me verse 3 of Psalm 148:

Praise ye him, sun and moon: praise him, all ye stars of light.

This Bible verse shows you that all nature delights in the God that made it. Delight in your God!

goodnight, Starry 1